Successful Women in Business

Edited by Jacqueline Rose

Research by: Sarah Chapman, James Morgan, Katerina Smith, Gregory Blackman and Olivia Cartwright.

Published by Lovely Silks Publishing 2016

Successful Women in Business

My voice is often soft but the words I say are strong. After all, women having opinions is a wonderful thing that can only benefit us all.

Junko Kemi - From The Boardroom To The Catwalk

Life is good, not because I'm jet setting around the world but because when I come home, I do so to a loving family. A home of giggles, happy children and a husband that appreciates the life we have together, a real man who loves my children like his own, and in laws that mean the world to me.

Lorena Öberg - From Self-Doubt To Self-Accomplishment

Life is indeed unpredictable and forever changing, but it also offers endless opportunities for those who are ready to embrace them. So make sure you are ready.

Suzi Chen - Curating Your Success

Don't forget to Embrace-Life, Love and Each Other.

Rosie Shalhoub – Embracing Rosie

Stay focused on what you believe in. It sounds obvious, maybe a little cheesy, but I have often repeated this mantra to myself over the years, especially when things get tricky.

Emma Coleman - From Nurse to Holistic Skin Specialist

We have built up a very recognisable brand, and by some referred to as an institution. This has been achieved through dedication, hard work and a passion for educating others and ourselves, not being afraid to fail and being innovative.

Linda Stewart – More Than Just A Salon

My journey has taught me to be flexible with my business and not to become too attached to any expectations. Expectation limits growth.

Melissa Aguirre - Beads, Yoga, & Chai! Oh My!

In order to grow a successful business, you will need to work on the business. If you are only working in the business, then all you have is a JOB.

Stacey Huish - The Why, The What & The How

Whilst it is crucial to work towards a healthy profit margin if a business is to make a change in the world for good, that company must have a healthy perspective on what will benefit its customer, its suppliers and the community at large.

Judith Treanor - Profit Or Purpose And Personal Fulfilment?

Starting a business with not much money is an achievable and rewarding path to success. Anyone that believes in themselves, and believes in their goals, like I did, can find their way into their own exciting venture. Find your own genius and create value for other people and you will find yourself skyrocketing to success.

Catherine Craig -Starting A Business With No Money

Learn To Celebrate Yourself - guess what? You are not perfect. And you know what? You don't have to be. Learn to accept yourself and love yourself. Don't beat yourself up for all your failures and weaknesses instead; celebrate your strengths and successes.

Christine Khor - Create the Life You Want

Word of mouth is another free way to market your business and it adds the benefit of trust. Friends and loyal customers will praise you and your products if you do right by them and give them great value.

Roberta Perry - Building Relationships And Getting Free Press For Your Business

Now I define "success" differently. Success for me is a general level of happiness and contentment in my daily life. Success is sleeping well at night, knowing that tomorrow is a new day filled with new possibilities.

Rebecca Carroll-Bell - Finding Out What Being Successful Really Means

Plan your days, weeks, months, quarters and year. Start with writing your top 5 goals for the year, and then break them down to small steps over the coming months, weeks and days. Believe in yourself, set realistic goals – enjoy the journey, not just the end result.

Kiran Singh - Design the Lifestyle You Desire

Always remember, there is not wrong way to run a business. Seek your opinion and talk to the right people. You only live once so live it without any regrets.

Sandra Yeow - 4 Lessons on How to Increase Success Rates for Any Start-up

I will always be looking for the opportunity. I have a list on my cork board that shows me the companies I want to do business with next to keep me motivated.

April Morse - Hard Times, Creative Thinking

We need to know our worth and that generally it is the woman and mother keeping the family unit together by taking care of the family. Sounds old school but it is generally how a family functions. Which is why we need to be full of love, to take care of ourselves and then others.

Renee Catt - Defining Success

Don't give up just because you failed, use that failure as momentum to learn and keep pushing forward.

Samantha R. Strazanac – Failing Your Way to Success

The thought leaders who contributed to this book:

Junko Kemi - From The Boardroom To The Catwalk

Lorena Öberg - From Self-Doubt To Self-Accomplishment

Rosie Shalhoub - Embracing Rosie

Emma Coleman - From Nurse to Holistic Skin Specialist

Linda Stewart - More Than Just A Salon

Melissa Aguirre - Beads, Yoga, & Chai! Oh My!

Stacey Huish - Successful Women In Business - The Why, The What & The How

Judith Treanor - Success: Profit Or Purpose And Personal Fulfilment?

Catherine Craig - Starting A Business With No Money

Christine Khor - Create the Life You Want

Rebecca Carroll-Bell - Finding Out What Being Successful Really Means

Kiran Singh – Design The Life Your Desire

Sandra Yeow - 4 Lessons on How to Increase Success Rates for Any Start-up

Roberta Perry - Building Relationships And Getting Free Press For Your Business

April Morse - Hard Times, Creative Thinking

Samantha R. Strazanac - Failing Your Way to Success

Suzi Chen - Curating Your Success

Renee Catt - Defining Success

Gems Inside

Welcome to Successful Women in Business

Women entrepreneurs are rarely satisfied with the status quo: Instead they strive to build the world in the way it should be rather than abiding by a system that's potentially archaic or outdated. During the course of researching this book we have come to realise that breaking down barriers for women in the workplace is key to success for companies and for countries.

That's the message we hope you will pick up from this book. When more and more women are seen at the top of organisations and running high growth technology businesses, the more this will be regarded as the standard and a perfectly normal, and logical, path to choose.

Starting a company, or managing a company through a period of transition and growth, can be a riveting roller coaster of emotions with tremendous highs and at times, difficult lows. But despite the challenges, many women have risen to become leaders and influential figures in their respective areas. Successful Women In Business recognizes and celebrates the outstanding contribution made by individual women to their businesses and, in many cases, their local communities. The business leaders profiled in this book are of various ages, social backgrounds and industries. However, the one common thread which unites them is that they dared to believe. And, in believing, they made the seemingly impossible a reality.

Their individual stories tell of the challenges we all face: uncertainty, fear, discouragement, hope, commitment and yes, that indefinable, illogical and yet all-consuming belief that we will succeed against all odds. These are real-life individual stories of success that I hope will also encourage you to believe - and to make that difference.

Jacqueline

Jacqueline Rose, Lovely Silks Publishing

From The Boardroom To The Catwalk

Humble beginnings

Ever since I was a little girl, I've always wanted to be my own boss, and the responsibility of having my own company excited me. I wanted to lead and inspire others to create new and innovative products that would make people happy and put a smile on their faces; I wanted to create 'new value'.

As a youngster, I didn't have a definitive plan of what my business would look like but looking back I guess it was obvious that I would enter the retail sector. After all, I was following in the footsteps of my beloved grandmother, who had the most influence on me becoming a businesswoman. Growing up, I spent a lot of time with my grandmother in her kimono shop in Osaka. She was kind, never complained, always helped others and achieved anything and everything she put her mind to - in short I thought she was so cool and wanted to be just like her.

As a retailer, customers appreciated her honesty and her flexible style of working for example, convenient opening hours and custom made clothes. With a child's enthusiasm, I would pretend that I was a customer walking around the shop, looking at how she could improve the business, from what suited customers to the colours and design of the fabrics adorning every shelf. Although she always listened to me she did not always take my advice.

Teenage struggles and finding my voice

The teenage years are a struggle for a lot of young people and sadly I was no exception. When I was around 14 or 15 years old, I failed to gain a place into my first choice high school (ages 12-18) and disliked my substitute choice. Whilst I can look back now and see that everything worked out for the best, at the time, this was devastating news for me, especially in the academically competitive environment of Japan. I lost a lot of confidence in myself, felt I wasn't good enough, didn't believe in my abilities and consequently really withdrew into myself.

I, like many teenage girls, placed a lot of pressure on myself, to succeed at everything I did and to fit in with my peers. The turning point for me came when I was 18 and one of my closest friends passed away from cancer. During our friendship, he provided me with much needed support, gave me confidence, believed in my abilities and told me that I was unique. At his funeral, I suddenly realised that life is far too short and that it passes by very quickly. I knew that I needed to be more confident, and concluded that for me to achieve my goals, the most important thing was to grab every opportunity and work as hard as I possibly could. Armed with this new attitude, my life changed for the better.

Shortly after, I began my degree at Waseda University studying Western History. While I was at university, I began hosting charity fundraisers and awareness events relating to the prevalence of HIV in Japan. This was a very topical and sensitive issue at the time due to a series of high-profile medical accident cases in which a group of young people were infected with HIV. Organising these events helped me to find my own voice, as I felt empowered by playing a part, even if it was a small part, in ensuring that students were better informed and in turn, better protected.

Entering the world of work

Upon graduation, my first job was with as a sales representative with Benesse, an education publishing company, in Osaka. Whilst I had a burning desire to establish my own company, I used this role to develop my basic skills and learn as much as I could in the areas of sales and marketing. By suggesting ideas for schools to tailor products to their students based on feedback from educational professionals, I was able to grow and be very creative in this role.

This experience of acting on customer feedback would prove invaluable in setting up my own companies in the future. My confidence at this time grew considerably and helped me gain real life skills. I went from being a total City girl to traveling around remote parts of Japan by myself and learning how to progress in a very male-dominated environment.

Aged 25, I decided that I wanted a new challenge, and I made the decision to leave Benesse for a role at the professional services firm, PwC. The nature of PwC meant that I learnt new skills in areas as diverse as accountancy, law and consulting, and my marketing skills came in handy as well! A short turnaround on projects became the norm, meaning I had to become adept at learning, accessing and analysing quickly on the job. The time I was at PwC was certainly an opportunity in which I was able to grow and solidify my experience and skills.

I've always believed that it is important to continually challenge yourself and your capabilities, so I decided to branch out further at Boston Consulting Group (BCG). As one of the biggest consulting firms in the world, BCG was the ideal place for me to learn more about the processes of business and to work alongside individuals from all walks of life, cultures and disciplines.

Initially, I found the role a challenge as I was working primarily in the medical and IT industries – a real departure from the education sector. However, I was ready for the challenge and excited at the opportunities to grow both professionally and personally. BCG's mantra is how to get maximum results in the shortest amount of time, which is crucial when you are working under tight deadlines and to high expectations. This was a useful learning point when I established my first business as I suddenly realised I would have to multi-task like I had never multi-tasked before.

Becoming my own boss

My boss at BCG was a very smart man, and he had observed and met many professionals in his time. He explained to me that my strengths were in marketing. Coming from someone with so much experience and high standards, these words were very powerful for me and helped me to formulate my future plan. Another former colleague encouraged me to take steps to find new clients, stating that once I had found three, I should resign from BCG. I took her advice and began to identify potential clients through my networks and social media. Soon, I had three clients, in IT, insurance and energy. After a lifetime of imagining and preparing, I started my own marketing consultancy business in 2008, five years after I joined BCG.

Starting again

I loved owning my own business – yes, it was incredibly hard work with lots of travelling and even more late nights but, seeing my business thrive and grow was the most rewarding feeling in the world. The company was called 'Maojian Works,' which is Chinese for my family name 'Kemi'. The reason I chose a Chinese name was because I had identified areas of growth for my business being outside of Japan, with China being a future key region.

On Friday 11th March 2011, my life completely changed. That day, I was in Nagoya, in the middle of a presentation to a client. The day was the day of the Great East Japan Earthquake and tsunami. The Tohoku earthquake once again made me realise how short life is, and after running my marketing consulting business for five years, I began reflecting on a piece of advice my grandmother gave me, "life is not about how much you make; it's about what you leave behind."

With this in mind, I thought of ways in which I could improve the lives of other women while also tapping into my interests and passions. An idea took hold based around the fact that I would often struggle to find clothes that worked with my busy professional life. You may not think it would be difficult to find practical and comfortable yet also elegant clothing in a city as large as Tokyo, I would spend my precious free time walking around malls and department stores for suitable work attire, only to return home empty handed. I wondered why the larger clothes companies were not catering to the professional female demographic and it was this moment that kay me, a fashion brand for businesswomen by a businesswoman was born.

Buoyed by excitement and a newfound energy, I began in earnest to answer two key questions - how do I produce a dress? And how do I ensure that women buy kay me dresses? My friends, who have been incredibly supportive, recommended a tailor and his advice was to collaborate with an excellent pattern cutter. Through the power of social media, I was introduced to a wonderful pattern cutter who not only creates beautiful garment templates but also has connected me to a wide range of industry professionals, suppliers and trading companies. She has and continues to be imperative to the kay me journey and I am proud to say she is now a partner in kay me.

During this time, I liaised with my network to hold focus groups, where I interviewed future kay me customers and showed them samples of potential products. This included an event at my former employer, Benesse where I presented the first collection to my fellow professional women and received some very useful and honest feedback. Feedback on areas including price and design was extremely valuable and helped me to shape and refine the collection, ensuring that the samples met all their requirements.

In my opinion, focus groups are extremely important and a valuable way of gaining insights from your core audience. However, if you are asking for advice it is important that you listen to any feedback given whether it is positive or not. It is never easy to listen to criticism; it does usually help the business in the long run.

By May 2011, just eight weeks after I had initially contacted the tailor, I had 40 samples and was fortunate enough to hold a launch party at a luxury hotel in Tokyo. Using my marketing skills, I was able to attract a large crowd with all of my dresses selling out on that first day. As you can imagine, I was delighted – a real highlight of the kay me journey so far.

In July 2011, I opened a showroom and invited customers to book appointments to view the collection. The showroom was located in an area close to Tokyo's financial district, making it easy for professional women to come and view the clothes at a convenient time for them. The showroom was so successful that after two months, I created an ecommerce platform and delivery service.

In 2012, kay me took a significant step forward when I opened my first bricks and mortar retail store in Ginza, Tokyo. Ginza is one of the most exclusive areas in Tokyo, equivalent to London's Mayfair or Fifth Avenue in New York and as a result, it was risky to launch in such a high profile and expensive area. However, it was vital that kay me launched in an area, which reflected our target audience, and I was so proud when the shop opened in September. Since then we have gone from strength to strength in Japan, and now have five bricks and mortar outlets. In addition to our flagship store in Ginza, we now have one in downtown Osaka, another at Haneda international airport and concessions in two Tokyo department stores.

Going International

2016 has been the year that we have really started to focus on expanding our horizons internationally. London was first on our agenda due to its talent pool, multiculturalism and the access it gives to other global cities including New York and Singapore (both of which are also on our hit list).

The first thing I have learned about how to launch in a new territory is to get the input and advice of people who are native to the country you are planning to launch in, because they will be able to provide insights into the local culture that you might miss. The second is to get feedback from your customer base – via everything from pop up shops to business pitching events - and don't assume that what worked for your brand at home will work in another country.

The third is that where English is a common language, the power of social media and an e-commerce platform enables you to tap into new territories without any 'boots on the ground' in the early stages. This being said, I don't think there is anything better than immersing yourself into the location and lives of your target audience.

This year I have spent a lot of time in London, and this has really opened my eyes to a different way of doing business and living life. By attending professional networking events and observing my target audience as they go through their working days – from pre-work work-outs to drinks with their team on a Thursday evening – I have learned a huge amount.

I will use this to adapt and improve our strategy for kay me in the UK, as well as cherry picking some of the areas that I most admire - efficient communications, prioritising team bonding time and regarding even leisure time as an opportunity to network - and see if they can be incorporated into the DNA of kay me's company culture back in Japan.

My top tips to anyone looking to launch their business into a new territory are: use your common sense; listen to everything and everybody's opinions, but also work with local experts; see the reality for yourself; be humble – you cannot know everything about a country you have only visited on holiday a few times; learn to localise your brand.

Lessons Learnt

Since launching kay me, one of my biggest challenges has been the transition from a business-to-business (b2b) to a business-to-consumer (b2c) organisation. In particular, I have found communicating, promoting and positioning my brand to a consumer rather than business audience to be a key learning.

For example, during kay me's first two years, stylists for newsreaders would often buy kay me to be worn on-screen. Soon after, we were approached by many stylists requesting dresses for TV drama roles.

The roles were varied, with some being a good fit for the brand, however, most did not reflect kay me customers who are hardworking businesswomen, often juggling multiple demands simultaneously. Upon reflection, we decided to be much more selective when working with TV production companies as their characters and viewers were not always representative of the kay me customer.

From this I learnt the importance of consistently reflecting your brand's message across all platforms and to ensure everybody at kay me understands the core messages at the heart of the brand. This continues to be an area for further growth for kay me, but I see this as an exciting challenge, rather than a daunting prospect.

It is also imperative that you have a financial safety net in place. Often people ask me how I was able to get kay me up and running in such a short space of time and without any major financial backing. The answer is that throughout my career I was always mindful of having reserve funds for when I finally branched out on my own.

Between 2008 and 2011, I managed to save most of my earnings from consulting for future investment. I knew that the consulting role was just a platform for something bigger, something greater, so it made sense to put something aside for the day when that came. The moment kay me launched, however, the bills started to come in thick and fast!

 Another important lesson I've learnt during my career is that anything really is possible and a positive learning can come out of difficult life experiences. All experiences, good or bad shape us and I would like to think looking back, my teenage friend would be proud of all my achievements and how much I've grown in confidence since we were 18.

Networking is also incredibly important. Without established on and off line networks in place, I would have really struggled to establish kay me as quickly and as successfully as I did. I have been lucky in that I've always admired my bosses and colleagues as they were very smart and always focused, and it has been a pleasure for me to keep in contact with them.

As a team leader now myself, I strive to inspire other young people in a similar way and as a result have established complementary English-for-business classes for all employees. Not only does this help them engage with customers traveling from overseas, but it also enables them to develop both professionally and personally, as language skills will be useful for the rest of their lives.

A piece of advice I would give particularly to younger readers is to travel. See the world. Have adventures. I really regret not traveling more when I was younger, as when I did start traveling abroad, I realised that I learnt so much about myself by meeting others who culturally were so different from me.

As I have expanded kay me internationally, I've also encountered a big learning curve in communicating with people in different languages.

Finally, I created kay me for businesswomen so that they could look and feel great and with this in mind, my final piece of advice is that as women, we should be strong, proud and not be fearful to share our opinions with others. My voice is often soft but the words I say are strong.

After all, women having opinions is a wonderful thing and can only benefit us all.

Junko Kemi

About The Author

Junko Kemi began her career as a salesperson for one of Japan's leading educational service providers, Benesse. From there, she worked as a marketing consultant for PwC and Boston Consulting Group.

In these roles, she developed a passion for sales and providing cost effective solutions for corporate institutions.

It was during this time that the foundations for the concept of kay me were born as she began to feel the need for a better mix of professional attire that could also be appropriate for after-work wear, entertaining clients or eating out with colleagues.

After launching in 2011, kay me how has five Japanese locations (a flagship store in Ginza, a store in downtown Osaka, another at Haneda international airport and concessions in two Tokyo department stores). Junko also launched kay me in London in the Summer 2016.

Website: https://www.kayme.co.uk

Twitter @kaymetokyo

Instagram @kaymetokyo

Facebook kaymelondon

Self-Doubt to Self-Accomplishment - Lorena Öberg's Story

Like most successful people, the seeds of who I am today started in early childhood. Being born into a highly dysfunctional middle class family has shaped the very nature of who I am and how I live my life today.

My mother handed me over to my nanny as soon as she brought me back from the hospital. My nanny Dina, as we know her to this day, took on full parenting roles. It was nanny Dina who did the school runs, made sure my homework was done and who took me to doctor's appointments. Still, this part of my early life was quite happy and stable. We lived with my maternal grandmother and my father, who by this time divorced from my mother, visited daily. The seeds to my self-esteem were sewn during this time and I credit this early stability and unconditional love for much of my success.

This all changed at the age of 8. My mother, for reasons that are still a mystery, decided to move the family to the city where my oldest sister lived. She unceremoniously fired my beloved nanny and put my grandmother in a nursing home leaving in her wake the lives of those that had served her for so many years. My father was devastated although he lost no time taking refuge in the arms of various unsavoury women soon forgetting both his sorrows and sadly mine.

My mother's new life was a disaster. It was the first time I'd lived with my oldest sister, 22 years my senior. My sister was 30 and, like my mother, took a liking to married men. At such an early age I could never have realised that my sister had been abandoned in a boarding school at the age of 5 and mother never visited. Like me, my sister was a very much unwanted child. Mother was 15 when she had her and was in her late thirties when I arrived. My sister unconsciously thought that I was my mother's favourite and of course, my mother wasted no time in playing us off against each other. I absolutely stood no chance against this grown woman who took huge gratification in seeing tears rolling down my eyes. The entire time my mother looked on with delight, she had found the perfect puppet to do her dirty work.

My daily needs where nowhere, on the scale of my mother's list of priorities, her main priority was her married lover and her second was travelling. If I dared to ask for clothes to replace the ones I had grown out of, I would be told that I was too fat and that if I lost weight they would fit me. If I needed money for school supplies, I was made to grovel after a telling off for not making my pencils last longer. The message I was sent was clear "You're an inconvenience in my life".

I went to University at 24, partly because I didn't have a job that paid well enough until then and partly because years of being told I was stupid and lazy had taken a toll of how I viewed myself. Everything I had ever tried to do had been sabotaged.

I funded my studies by working full time. Once at university, I went to lectures during the week and worked ten-hour shifts on Friday, Saturday and Sunday. But it wasn't long, before I began to do well. This was a revelation because I believed I was stupid. Soon, I was in the honour roll and for the first time in my life I had the respect of my peers. I put myself through all sorts of self-tests trying to convince myself that I was actually intelligent. By the time I graduated, I had finally proven my family wrong. I was intelligent and capable of anything. From then on, no one would be able to make me believe differently.

Although my self-esteem would never again be compromised, my boundaries were another story. I had very low expectations of how people should treat me. I had been raised in an environment where promises were not kept and questions were met with conflict. In short, I had learnt to expect NOTHING from ANYONE. I figured out that true happiness comes from within, and in my case happiness came from living my life in a way I thought was honourable. I tried to do what I believed to be right and live my life with what I now know is called integrity.

Sadly, low self-worth had landed me in a marriage with a man with traits very much like my mother. I have to admit that this didn't bother me very much as I had the coping mechanisms to deal with drama and everything being blamed on me. For years I was happy, and even more so when my two wonderful children were born. I understood that to keep the peace in my marriage, just as I had done growing up, I had to have no expectations of anything.

I worked full time to pay the bills and to give my children everything they needed. My husband just paid the mortgage and only the mortgage. This is what he said married couples did, and to be honest, it was not worth the argument so I complied. Staying quiet during conflict seemed to be my only defence. I never saw my girlfriends because for me to go out was not worth the backlash when I got home. Although he didn't do much to help with the children he was and is a good father. He played with them and indulged their every whim. The children would talk AT him for hours well beyond the point where most parents would scream SILENCE! Yet he had and still has the patience of a saint!

The marriage, infidelities, lies, and the constant struggle of having all of the responsibilities, financial and otherwise, were wearing me down. Being with a controlling man, who would start an argument if I took too long to wash my hair and whose spending was out of control, left me feeling trapped. But it wasn't until I saw him trying to manipulate my 6 year old daughter that I was compelled to start making a change.

I went online to try to figure out what to do. Amongst my many searches and vast research, I came across a condition known as Narcissistic Personality Disorder. Suddenly there was an explanation for everyone and everything throughout my entire life. The pattern of abuse, the infidelities, the self-serving behaviours, the lies and being blamed for everything, it finally all made sense. The more I researched the subject the more I saw the pieces of the puzzle fit together. It was then I realised that my situation could never get better, that the people around me would never change and that the only person who can change my children's future, and mine, was me.

The final straw came after an altercation between us, which took place in front of friends, and the next day when I came home from work I found him sulking trying to spin the incident to be my fault. I had no more fight left in me; he had taken every last bit of energy I had to keep our marriage together and to try to give our children a happy home. Instead of trying to appease him, this time, I asked him to leave and this time there was no turning back. I wanted a divorce and there would be no reconciliation, or any promises of another a holiday. This time, it was over, in my heart, in my soul, it was over. He soon left declaring that he was getting nothing from our marriage and that no one would ever want me. I was past the point of caring who wanted me, my only focus was providing a good life for my children. Then from the moment he walked out that door I began my detox.

Anyone that was not contributing in a positive way to my life had to go. My last conversation with my sister had been years before when she put the phone down on me declaring that she would never speak to me again. In my heart, I had always left that door open in case one day, she wanted to resume contact. But this time, I closed that door for good.

I have to admit that when my husband left I felt a huge amount of relief. Whilst we were together I had been as good a single mother the entire time, but now without the constant stress of possible conflict, it was bliss. We had agreed verbally how assets were going to be split so that the children could stay in the family home. We had agreed to wait for two years before filing for divorce and that he would continue to pay for the mortgage, this happened for only a few months. Soon I began to get letters telling me the mortgage wasn't being paid and that he had used our home as security to take out large loans. It became apparent to me that he was trying to bankrupt me and ruin my credit, I had no choice but to proceed with filing for divorce.

His revenge came after the children wanted to spend a week with him and a week with me. This arrangement can work very well when both parents are doing it for the interest of the children, but I knew this wouldn't be the case. I had evidence to prove he was doing it to leverage a better financial settlement out of me and to pay less child support. I knew beyond a shadow of a doubt that if I had full custody of the children, they would grow up to have a close relationship with both parents. But I knew him, if he had them half the time, they could be used as pawns in our divorce.

I found myself faced with a high court battle and no money to cover solicitor fees. So I did the only thing that I could do, I quit my job, and went on government benefits, got ready to lose the only home my children had ever known, all to make fighting for my children my full time job. I was confident that I had right on my side, I self-represented. I would show up to court on my own to face him and his barrister, and believed I would come out of that courtroom with what I wanted and what was fair for my children and I, because I had right on my side.

The fight went on for three and a half years, and it was during this time that I had to come up with a way of supporting my children. I needed to find something I could do around my children and their routines, especially as they were so little, only 5 and 7. The thought of living from government funds and raising my children in that way terrified me but with my husband dragging out the divorce, it was difficult to say the least. Then one day a doctor friend of mine said to me "why don't you try tattoo removal, you'd be good at that". They turned out to be the most prophetic words any person has ever said to me.

I immediately began researching tattoo removal and the numbers stacked up. I found Dermace Training Academy near Leeds, so I took the plunge. I also trained in Medical and Cosmetic Tattooing at the same time, and put it all on credit cards. At that point in my life I thought I would have to file for bankruptcy, so I figured I may as well have a new career from it. I never did have to file for bankruptcy and my gut instinct was right about my new career.

I then made it my mission to be successful, I got busy writing a business plan and making a website. I made a website myself because I had no money to hire anyone. I also knew a bit about ranking on Google and SEO (search engine optimisation) so I put all my skills into action. Still, I was broke, and without any money I couldn't rent a premises and without a premises, I didn't have a business. I heard through the grapevine that a local hair salon had a beauty room to rent. I immediately went to speak to the owner, and used money from my credit cards to put down my first deposit. That day I remember with great fondness, not only was that the beginning of my business but it was the day I met my now husband.

So I began my self-employed journey but with no money to advertise, business was slow. I advertised in all the free places I could and prayed that someone would see it. Early on I told myself that I had a full time job. If I wasn't treating someone, I was working on marketing. One such day, I was home working on marketing with the television on in the background and it came to me, *"If lasers worked like this, and micro-needling worked like that….if I used them together in this way….wouldn't that work for stretch marks?"*

At that time, my body was covered in stretch marks. I pulled out my equipment, used a lot of numbing cream and away I went. I nearly fainted a few times but I completed my treatment, and a month later my stretch marks were greatly reduced. I then called all my friends to trial it on them; they all had great results too. I knew I had something special, and so, **DermaEraze** was born.

I had a couple of bespoke treatments to offer. I had tattoo removal, permanent makeup and stretch marks as specialist treatments under my belt. The problem was that no one knew about me and with no money to advertise I thought I was doomed. The salon owner didn't allow me to put anything in the window so walk through trade was out of the question but my website was ranking a bit better. Until one day I received a phone call from a journalist who was writing an article about stretch mark treatments and asked if she could come try my treatment and write about it. She wrote a very honest article, and despite of her complaints about how much it hurt, she told the truth, and how it worked.

I was working between school runs, an irregular client flow and struggling to pay the rent for the treatment room. Stefan, my now husband pointed out the financial difficulties in all sorts of graphs, which I could barely see through my tears. I knew that if I didn't do well, I wouldn't be able to feed my kids, and if I did well, my ex-husband would try to go after my business. He had already tried to ruin my credit and make us homeless, so at this point nothing would have surprised me.

One day I received a phone call from Groupon asking if I wanted to run a deal for Permanent Makeup. The numbers didn't make sense and so I declined.

Then I asked them if they would run a deal on stretchmark's. We went through the numbers and we were able to come up with a deal that made sense. The deal ran and we sold 175 Groupons. Overnight, I was solid with clients for eight hours a day! Some upgraded to larger areas some didn't but it didn't matter because I was getting my name out there. Soon Wowcher contacted me and we did the same. These relationships lasted years and although my business is now at a point where we no longer run deals, I will forever be grateful to those two companies. They did the marketing for me at a point when I simply could not afford to advertise. My advice to anyone who believes these companies charge too much in commission is to negotiate and structure the proposed deals to accommodate both parties' interests.

I soon realised that putting all my eggs in the daily deal basket was dangerous and I wanted to stand out and promote my treatments through the press so I took on a PR agency. I showed them that article about DermaEraze and told them I had something really special, we agreed on a fee that I could afford and got started with PR.

Taking on PR was a huge leap of faith. I remember asking if they really thought I would get press coverage. My self-doubt was fuelled by the ghosts of my past telling me that I was useless, stupid and incapable of ever succeeding. My PR sensed this and the next day in the post was a book called "The Secret". When I received it I thought it was a business book when I read it I realised it was so much more. That book taught me how to stop self-sabotaging. It taught me to change my thought pattern from self-doubt to empowerment. It didn't happen overnight but I began my internal detox. The first step was to, again, get rid of the toxic people in my life, but the most important step was to get rid of what they left behind. I will always be a product of my up-bringing but today I choose to only hold on to the parts that make me extraordinary.

My PR told me I needed an address in London, preferably Harley Street, I told them they were crazy and I could barely afford the premises I had. Still, something clicked and I grabbed my kids and went off to Harley Street, walking into 1 Harley Street and asked them if they rented rooms by the hour. They said they did, and so, we got busy booking in my first press days.

From those press days, I began to get busy in London and six months later I had to take full time residence at number 1 Harley Street. I'm still there and am still very happy.

During this time I was doing something I had no idea about it was so pioneering in the beauty and cosmetics industry. When my clients came in for Permanent Makeup, often they would come in with old work that I couldn't tattoo over. I would suggest to my clients that I laser off their old work and start fresh. In the beginning I relied on test patching, figuring out how different pigments reacted under the laser and reading as many medical journals as I could get my hands on. I am fully insured to work on the face so it never occurred to me that it couldn't be done.

One day someone added me to a Facebook group for Permanent Makeup Artists. I lurked for a while because by this time I had been in the beauty industry for two years and had worked in a very insular way so knew no one from the industry.

At first I was very reluctant to fraternise with my "competitors". What I saw was that my colleagues were posting photos of people with bad work, saying that they were "disfigured for life", and the whole time I was thinking *are you kidding me, put her under my laser and I'll have her good to go in three treatments*.

By the time anyone told me that lasers didn't work on removing permanent makeup, I had been successfully doing it for years. I remember responding to a photo about this that was posted in one of the groups so I replied with series of ten before and after photos. I had been using custom made lasers. This is when people really started to take notice. I began to get messages asking if I could train people. I dismissed this at first but after the tenth message I thought, I can do this and so I did.

I was soon asked to speak at a large conference. After that, other conferences followed and soon, somehow, I became the go to person for the removal of permanent makeup. What I didn't realise, in that little room inside a hair salon, was that I was doing something that no one else thought possible within the industry. I didn't know it couldn't be done, so I just did it.

I soon got asked to speak at a Permanent Makeup Conference, and then another and another. I began to get asked to teach in America and so my lasers had to go through all the legal hoops there. I now teach all over the world and speak to hundreds of people about removing pigment from the face safely.

Today, my husband and I run two very busy clinics. Celebrities seek me out for my skin rejuvenation and other bespoke treatments. People travel from all over the world to have treatments with us and DermaEraze is being rolled out to clinics worldwide allowing women from all over to benefit from it. I am in high demand for speaking and teaching across the globe. To this day I am still so taken back when I get asked to speak at conferences and pass on my advice. People are interested in what I have to say and wish to learn from me. However, this is not what makes me successful.

True success can only be achieved when one reaches a point in their lives where they are happy. Any child of abuse will tell you that the one thing we want above everything else is a loving family. My divorce is long over and the children are still close to their father. Three years ago Stefan and I got married on the day that was my mother and father in law's 50th wedding anniversary. In the same little medieval church they walked down the aisle 50 years earlier.

My mother and father in law are the parents I never had who love and respect me and dote on our children. When I'm on television or I win an award, it's my mother in law that calls to congratulate me. They are the ones that fly in to help us with the children during school holidays. Through them I have learnt that the only thing that is thicker than water is love.

I now live a life without drama. No huge ups or downs. No one uses guilt to control me. My children taught me that in order for them to be happy, I have to be happy first. I have achieved my goals and desires to make sure they did not have the life I'd broken free from.

Life is good, not because I'm jet-setting around the world but because when I come home, I do so to a loving family. I come home to giggles, happy children and a husband that appreciates the life we have together, a real man who loves my children like his own, and in laws that mean the world to me.

Lorena Öberg

About The Author

Lorena Öberg is a world-renowned Skin Repair Expert, CEO and Founder of Lorena Öberg Skincare.

Based in London's prestigious Harley Street and Surrey, Lorena offers patients specialist treatments for various skin conditions using pioneering techniques, including tattoo removal, semi-permanent make up correction and migration.

Lorena is also a pioneer in scar and stretch mark reduction and recently launched DermaEraze®, a unique technique that has been hailed in international press for its high success rates. Under her brand DermaLipo® Lorena also offers a highly acclaimed advanced body contouring, non-invasive ultrasonic liposuction, ultrasound inch-loss and skin tightening treatment, with proven results.

Lorena runs an international training academy where she uses her skills and abilities to teach the next generation. She regularly attends conferences and lectures across the globe and speaks about various topics ranging from industry trends, motivation, regulations and new techniques.

Lorena founded her successful business five years ago with £100 and having two young children to support. Lorena first discovered her talent after a friend suggested she tried tattoo removal. With a change in career she has never looked back.

In 2013 Lorena married Stefan Öberg and the couple live in Caterham Surrey with their family.

To find out more about Lorena Öberg Skincare and treatments visit:

www.lorenaoberg.co.uk

For further information or interview requests please contact Alliance PR

On: 020 7481 9444 or Rebecca@alliancepr.co.uk

Defining Success

To be a successful woman in business means many different things to each woman. Whether your take is financial success, or success based on your reputation or whatever you choose it to mean for you.

I choose to believe that being a successful woman in business means to be a business that contributes to others, that is game changing in an industry that comes from a place of heart and purpose. While allowing me to do what I am meant to do, to unleash my own inner brilliance and genius and do what I am passionate about. That then supports my life, my lifestyle and allows me to continue to be the best mum possible for my two children who are nearly 9 and 7 ½ years of age. That is the big version of being a successful woman in business.

Or I could say 'being a successful woman in business allows me to do what I want, when I want and how I want and that is for the benefit of me and others'.

Being in business for me prior to my life reboot of 2012, I had been in the travel industry for 15 years. A job I loved and worked very hard at and a job that had a lot of stress to it also. I ran this business from home once I fell pregnant in 2007 and it enabled me to have an amazing lifestyle working from home. It allowed me to fully love and enjoy both my pregnancies and be able to relax with the changes more so than if I had to rush into work and was concerned about being late.

I loved working from home and being my own boss and being able to network and attend events when I wanted to. I was able to work when the babies were asleep and work fitted into my routine and the kid's schedules. Running my business from home also meant that when my marriage ended and I was finding it hard to focus, that I could take the time off I needed. I could step away from the desk and get fresh air when I needed.

Then being a single mum and running my own business from home felt rather daunting and scary but then empowering at the same time. For the last 4 years I have been able to do this. I have been able to be at the school when I needed to be and when my kid's E & K asked me to be present. So this for me, felt like success.

But something inside me wanted more. I knew that I wanted to be more than a 50 year old travel agent. There was a drive and a yearning inside my heart that wanted more. While I knew I could be happy going with the flow and continuing running the travel business from home, I had heaps of friends who were still loving and thriving. I just knew I wanted more but I had no idea what that was going to be or how I would do it. I simply did not know what I did not know.

Then I guess, sometimes like having the shakes, you awake and say: 'here is your wake-up call. You wanted more, here is the more you asked for.' It might not have exactly been how I wanted it, but I know that sometimes we don't get what we think we want, we get what we need. But we do get what we ask for....

My reboot and my 'more' took the shape of my marriage ending at a time in my life that I consider to be my version of rock bottom. I felt completely shattered and broken at the time. I felt alone, insignificant, confused, scared, worried, afraid, sad and was suffering high anxiety at the time. I did not recognise the woman I saw in the mirror. I did not like the way I was feeling. I was concerned about my future and the kid's future. How would I cope and survive? What had I done to deserve this? Why couldn't we make our marriage work for the sake of our family?

These are normal questions that go through your head at the time, but extremely un-empowering at the same time. Normal and ok. What would I do next?

Run off (well fly off) to the McLaren Vale and drink Shiraz for 4 days is what I did, while being supported by my dad and his wonderful wife, as this was where they lived - and what a place to 'drown my sorrows' so to speak. The kids stayed home with their dad while I had some much needed time out for me. It was here, in South Australia's finest wine country that I started to heal. I started my journey of searching for information that would help me figure out my next steps. It was wise words from Bev, my dad's wife, 'I think you need to accept your marriage is over and make new plans when you go home'.

So I did. I fumbled my way through most of it though. The Googling and talking to people, friends and others. Here were some clear steps forward, a check list of sorts that would show me what to do. It was much easier to get married, so why was it so hard to get un-married? Was I separating or was I getting a divorce, how does this all work and where is the right information? Surely it can't be that hard and do I really need to run off to a lawyer right now?

I had no idea what to do and actually, I did not want to do anything right now, I just wanted to be able to 'be' and sit with the feelings and emotions. Then I would get around to my next step forward. I went through the motions and focused on my own inner health so that I could be the best mum at the time for E & K. I did get some legal advice and then some more and then I was served papers for court. Talk about being rocked at your core and kicking you while you are down. That is how I felt at the time.

Then jump 12 months ahead, working away in the travel business and I have just come back from Las Vegas on my divorce holiday. All in the name of research. The travel business was focusing on health retreats and now I had an idea for divorce holidays. I was chatting to some industry colleagues not long after I had come back from a stunning health retreat in Thailand. I was getting comments on how great I looked and asked what I had done to heal. I knew that I needed to go on another solo holiday and go somewhere warm, where I could get pool side service, room service, where there was action and adventurous activities. I wanted to shop and go to day spas and then dance the night away. Where else in the world could I do this? Las Vegas of course. Being completely honest, I also wanted some attention and to get my flirt on. I was ready for that.

I was completely focused on the divorce holiday idea but also because I was being asked so often how I got over my divorce so well. I then wanted to help other women going through a separation and divorce too. But I wasn't a counsellor a psychologist or a coach. I was just little ole me, the girl next door. The girl next door still had that inkling inside that she wanted more. Again, I did not want to be a travel agent in 20 year's time, I had just turned

40 and still wanted more. Then while working away on the divorce holiday idea a business coach said to me, 'Renee, whenever you talk about helping others through their divorce, you light up, your voice changes.' Yes, I said. 'So, just go do that, be the Divorce Go To Girl'.

It was like someone had given me permission to go after what my heart was telling me to do, I just had to get my 'head' out of the way. Take all the logic aside and just follow my intuition and this yearning inside. It was like someone had turned a light on inside me. I have never looked back, only forward to all the possibilities.

Finding Purpose & Passion

However, it was not until I attended a workshop run by Carolyn Tate on "Purpose" that I realised I could actually change my career and start a business because I had found my purpose and my passion. I used to think 'doing what you love' is for sports' elite athletes or rock stars. I didn't think the 'girl next door' could do that. Wasn't I just supposed to 'get a job' and do that? Keep on keeping on with being a travel agent? Now, don't get me wrong I have loved the industry and understand it is a more challenging job than many people understand. I just wanted more.

I knew in my heart of hearts and felt with every bone in my body that helping others through their separation and divorce is what I wanted to do and just had to do. Trust me, working in this space, I have thought about quitting it many times. Hearing about all the hurt people do to each other at the end of the marriage, and during also, does make you want to cry. Then I think, how would I be fulfilled doing something else? Would 'x' job fill my cup up? Would I be making a bigger difference in the world? The answer is always no. I know that I must show people how to see the flip side to their separation and divorce.

When you work with people going through one of life's most challenging times, and the feedback is 'you are my earth angel' or even one lady was considering committing suicide one night when I spoke to her for a few hours. She is alive and well and seeking further help now. When you are up doing coaching until 1am because someone needs you that much (extremely rare) you know you are on purpose with what you are meant to do. This to me is success: doing what you are passionate about and that has a purpose.

Seeing people come through their separation and divorce a renewed version of who they are, and thought they were, is extremely fulfilling. To help others shortcut their time frame in how they feel about getting back into life is very rewarding. When women (and some men) learn how to see the opportunity in their new start is what lights me up. As they understand the roles they played in the relationship and how they got to where they are now, brings my clients to the place of acceptance, which is the first phase in true healing and moving forward.

People come to me in person or on line or on the phone and they are in a world of confusion, just like I was, and they have no idea where to even start with the whole process. Which is why I created my free online Beyond The Breakup Boot camps. To deliver a week's worth of information to help with their steps forward and then the emotions behind their feelings is how I contribute and give back to people in the early days of separation.

My mission and my why

Now jump 4 years on from my marriage ending and I feel like I have gone through my own 'tsunami of a divorce' and I can see a big gap in the market for helping couples separate successfully together, and stay out of court. From working with lawyers, mediators and the court system, I have experienced a lot.

My big mission now is to change the way 'we' as a country and society actually do separations and divorce. Mostly all of our actions and emotions come from a place of fear and other negative emotions like anger and resentment. No one really wants to talk about divorce, but I know we need to. We need to talk about it so we know we can do it better and differently. To divorce from a place of kindness, and exit the marriage or untie the knot just like we came into the marriage. Being civil and kind. I know, mixing those words into the divorce space doesn't really seem to match. That is a good thing.

We need to be authentically amicable and be focused on the best interests of our children. There needs to be a bridge to fill the gap between couples and their lawyers and help them deal with the emotional roller-coaster that lies ahead. Plus, what the right steps forward are. By educating, inspiring and empowering the individual and the couple to see their separation and divorce as an opportunity for a new beginning. To divorce with kindness, compassion and empathy.

The way we have been separating and divorcing is not helping those actually going through the process. Divorce costs the Australian Government 14 billion dollars a year.

http://www.news.com.au/lifestyle/relationships/marriage/divorce-is-costing-the-australian-economy-14-billion-a-year/news-story/e5a101ea76351d4ba145279011b934ac

However, the emotional costs outweigh the financial. We can make more money, but we can never get back time. Depression is also a common occurrence after a marriage ends and you are likely to go through very similar stages of grief as if someone had died. Sometimes this is even harder to deal with as this person is still in your life. So we need to encourage healthy relationships post separation. Women and men move on differently from each other because we are wired differently as humans. I do feel that we need to come together during this time and work out the separation together. No taking sides and fighting each other. We just have to have awareness and separate differently. For the sake of our children but also ourselves, our own healing and journey so we are the best parents for our children and our children's children.

What if we could end our marriage in a more 'aware' state and have the conversations we need to have with our partners, the way they need to had? Not with fighting through lawyers and the court system. What if we could take the emotions out, just for a bit, and focus on the future. Not what he did or she did and understand there are three sides to every story, his side, her side and the truth. That no one is really at fault or to blame. We all participated in the relationship.

The truth is we aren't taught how to have successful and lasting relationships. We definitely are not taught now to end them consciously either. As divorce rates rise to nearly 50% and then second marriages are around 75% divorce rate, wouldn't it be great if we did relationships differently and also spent time healing before we moved on?

My why continues on to be about my E & K, my wonderful kids and the legacy I am going to leave them. Before all that though, I need to be my best to be their best. I know many women after they have children, then put their children first. Which seems normal and the status quo. However, when we don't put ourselves first we then forget about our own needs and how we need to be filled up with love to be able to give our over flow to our children and partners. Without putting ourselves first, then a little bit of resentment builds and builds and bubbles over. We then start to feel unappreciated. None of this helps anyone. We need to know our worth and that generally it is the woman and mother keeping the family unit together by taking care of the family. Sounds old school but it is generally how a family functions. Which is why we need to be full of love, to take care of ourselves and then others.

With putting ourselves first, then comes finding the harmony between it all, or maybe that is balance for some, or just being flexible. Have a life which is in harmony and balance is when we are in flow and everything is all working as we would like. Which is why I find working for myself and doing what I want and when I want enables harmony and balance. It's knowing how to take care of that little rollercoaster rides of life that may happen along the way. That is what matters most, and again, when our love tank is full and we are taking care of ourselves first, we are able to deal with the ups and downs and sideways and this ways and that.

Taking care of our business, on all levels, whether they be spiritual, personal, professional, social and any other area you need to take care of, by filling all those areas of our life, is another version of success for me. Do these happen all at the same time? Mostly, but occasionally they are off balance, but that is ok, that is life. It is how we bounce back and fill up our own personal tanks that matters.

For me, this is what being a successful business woman is all about; Doing what I am meant to do and serving others from a place of love. A big mission, absolutely, will I need help sharing my message? Every day, all day.

Renee Catt

About The Author

After going through her own 'tsunami' of a divorce, Renee became known as the Divorce Go To Girl and is sought after for her expert advice on separation, divorce, and beginning again as a single mum. She was also labelled as a 'Divorce Guru' by Kiis FM and has been seen across many media publications.

Renee saw a gap in the market to help couples separate together, with kindness and now helps to bridge the gap between the unknown of separation, divorce and seeing a lawyer. Her company is called Separation Success.

She aims to change the way people view their divorce and how they separate and move forward. Bringing in her own strategies, other experts and being a qualified coach and mentor, Renee helps couples move through the emotional stages of their relationship ending as they know it, encouraging couples to maintain an authentically amicable relationship in the future.

If you would like to find out more, visit Renee's website at:

www.separationsuccess.com

Curating Your Success

I remembered it vividly.

The Secretary-General of the United Nations Ban Kim-moon was speaking to an audience primarily made up of young business men and women. I counted. I was 8 seats away from where he was standing. It was only a day earlier that I stood in the exactly same spot where the Secretary-General was standing as I facilitated a Summit session on the theme of young people and world peace.

I was at the United Nations Headquarters in New York City. Needless to say, my 2-day visit to the iconic place in July 2016 was a highlight for me both personally and professionally.

At 37 years old, I am a global business consultant, an award-winning graphic designer, a business writer, an international speaker and trainer and an avid traveller who happens to hold a long list of qualifications of which includes a doctoral degree.

I cannot say I planned to walk the career path that I am on right now as a lot of my accomplishments came as unexpected, but my accomplishments are not completely accidental. I attribute my success to a combination of having an innovative mind-set and a series of strategic manoeuvres, a powerful combination that has served me well.

Specifically, there are 5 strategic manoeuvres that I have benefitted from greatly throughout my career.

Manoeuvre 1: Don't fall into the trap of indecisiveness by asking yourself the "10 years' time" question.

People always find it interesting, some even gasps in surprise, when they find out my background. As a former medical scientist, I hold a doctoral degree and specialised in vascular medicine or study of blood vessels. People find it fascinating that I would abandon a hard-earned medical research career to embark on something totally different. At times I too find it hard to explain.

I do, however, remember the feeling that I had towards the end of my clinical research career. After years of working in hospital, I had nailed my routine and perfected the research procedures and techniques to a point that, if I was allowed, I could probably conduct my research with my eyes shut. As my work became a routine so was my restlessness.

I knew I had to make a change and that change was difficult. To start with, I worked very hard to become a doctor so I could contribute to scientific discovery; it was a noble career. I also had cultural pressure. As a young female Asian research doctor, I was seen by many as the one that others would inspire to. I had the brain and I had a respectable and intellectual job; it was almost a crime to give it all up to do something completely different. Of course, I knew I was not the first or only person to decide to change gear and start a new career path, but it certainly felt like that.

It was a simple question that took away my internal debates and cemented my resolve. I asked myself if I could see myself in the same position in 10 years' time. The answer was clear. The thought of being stagnant and remaining at the same spot in 10 years' time gave me the chill. So I began my transition and the rest is a history.

From time to time in our life, we are no doubt faced with challenging decisions. The uncertainty that the future holds naturally contributes to our agony of indecisiveness. I have come to learn that there is one question that sets me free from indecisiveness when I stand at a cross road and that is the "10 years' time" question.

Not sure if you should change your job, ask yourself the "10 years' time" question – *what happens if I am still doing the same job in 10 years' time?*

Not sure if you should spend the money and send your children on a costly overseas exchange program with school, ask yourself the "10 years' time" question – *what happens if my children do not have the required cultural competency and global perspective in 10 years' time?*

There are no right or wrong answers. The "10 years' time" question is merely a tool to minimise the unhelpful internal debates happening inside our head when facing a challenging situation. Rather than continuing the indecisiveness, it is better to approach a difficult decision in a logical manner. The "10 years' time" question does exactly that.

It may be that you are comfortable with seeing yourself holding the same job in 10 years' time. Perhaps the job is close to home and gives you financial stability and that is okay as we all want different things in life.

Maybe you are not in a position to send your children on an expensive overseas exchange program with school, but recognising the importance of globalisation has on today's society, perhaps you could explore other affordable cultural experiences for your children.

Whatever our answers are, the "10 years' time" question gives us some confidence in our decision-making process. Therefore, do remember to ask yourself the question from time to time so you do not fall into the trap of indecisiveness and live to regret it.

Manoeuvre 2: Don't fall into the trap of narrow-minded advice.

Part of my career transition was talking to recruitment agents and seeking their advice. One recruitment agent told me that my prospect of finding a decent position outside the medical field was not great. Her reasoning was based on the fact that my experience and skillsets up to this point were in a very niched area. In other words, by being specialised in the research area of blood vessel diseases meant that I was practically obsolete unless I remained in the scientific industry.

I thought that was absurd. The recruitment agent essentially was saying that one must be employed in the field of their chosen study. As I am a true believer that life is not a linear path but a convergent of my unexpected opportunities, I begged to differ.

So I thought about what other skills and experiences that I had that other industries apart from medicine would be interested in. I was glad the list was not a short one. In addition to my intellectual capacity and prior voluntary experience, I found others would appreciate my skills in general administration, project management and relationship building or even stakeholder engagement. All of these skills I applied during my time managing clinical research projects and these were the skillsets that my next employer valued the most.

Armed with my quiet self-confidence, I began the next phase of my career working as a project manager in the emergency management services sector. For the next 5 years, I had a lot of fun managing and delivering major projects that worth millions of dollars. It was also during this phase of my career that I experienced the strongest personal growth to date.

Had I listened to that well-meaning but narrow-minded recruitment agent, I would have never embarked on a journey of self-discovery and re-invention.

So take people's advice seriously, but do so with caution so you do not fall into the trap of narrow-minded advice.

Manoeuvre 3: Don't fall into the trap of linearity but be the one who can connect the dots.

I was delivering a keynote speech to members of the Golden Key Honour Society. As the world's largest collegiate honour society who only invites the top 15% of university students to be members, it is suffice to say that I was talking to a group of academically gifted young people.

The focus of the keynote speech was about building an inclusive and resilient community as the organiser wished to make an emphasis on the fact that life is more than just good grades. Understanding the fact that life is not just one dimension and being able to put things in perspective, or even better, being able to "connect the dots" is a crucial skill to a young person.

This, of course, applies to all of us who may have graduated from university or college long ago.

What does it mean to be able to "connect the dots" and why is it so important to business success? "Connecting the dots" comes from one's ability to identify opportunities by making sense of a multitude of information, often from unlikely places. It requires an agile and open mind and it requires one to be flexible. "Connecting the dots" is a skill that many entrepreneurs or innovators possess and a skill that Steve Jobs used to describe about creativity.

So how does one learn to connect the dots? In addition to having an open mind, having as many diverse experiences as possible is crucial. It is extremely difficult to make sense of situations if one does not have enough knowledge or experience to draw on. A wide range of experiences provides a fertile ground where fresh and often unexpected ideas are born. This is one of the reasons why young people tend to think one dimension, because they have a lack of life experience.

To ensure that I do not exhaust my "knowledge or experience bank", I make sure that traveling is built into my business plan so I can continue to accrue new experiences. I particularly love to combine business and travel together, because it is cost and time effective. I also pay attention to "dig a little bit deeper" when I travel, so I am not just a tourist but a traveller who actually experiences.

For instance, through my many trips to Japan I have come to know Onigawara or ogre tile, a special type of roof ornament found in Japanese architecture that "protects" a home from evil. I have also met the last Oni-shi or ogre tile artisan in eastern Japan, Shigeru Yamaguchi.

Knowing Mr Yamaguchi, who is a 5th generation artisan keeping this dying art form alive, has got my mind working overtime. I ask myself: *What opportunities exist in this instance that local communities and my company can work on to save this dying art?* While ideas have just begun to surface, this particular travel experience demonstrates the importance of having a "knowledge or experience bank" on our ability to innovate and connect the dots.

To be successful, we need to remember that we do not live life in a linear fashion. So make sure to go out there and fill up our "bank" with a wide range of experiences.

Go and live an enriched life!

Manoeuvre 4: Say no to the "shotgun" approach and be strategic about your growth and development.

As an ambivert, I enjoy people's company and can function well in social setting, but very often I actually prefer to work alone. Given my slightly anti-social tendency, I have learned early on in my career to put strategies in place to ensure I do not become totally disengaged and live happily ever after by myself in my own bubble. So when it comes to setting a growth and development strategy, I make sure it is a very focused one.

For example, I sit on the governing board of 2 non-profit organisations. Being a company director provides me with governance training and career credibility, it also means that "I am out there" minimising my anti-social tendency. Further, to maintain my connection with the medical and health industry, one of the organisations that I hold a company directorship for is a community health organisation.

I also make sure that I deliver at least 2 public lectures or workshops every year. This is to ensure that I do not shy away from public speaking and as a non-native English speaker, I continue to provide myself opportunities to hone my language skills.

Having an understanding of myself and by being strategic about my growth and development, I have enjoyed many exciting opportunities made available to me. These opportunities include facilitating a Summit session at the United Nations Headquarters in New York City for a non-profit organisation and being invited to deliver a business lecture on innovation in Japan.

Just like other aspects of our life, our growth and development strategy needs to be planned. Ideally, a growth and development plan that offers clarity has the following characteristics:

- It complements our long term goals.
- It addresses our areas of strengths by putting us slightly out of our comfort zone.
- It acts as a source of inspiration by giving us an opportunity to explore new things.

So one should take their time when it comes to planning for a growth and development strategy. Make sure the strategy takes a focused rather than a "shotgun" approach and covers the above mentioned characteristics.

With a strong growth and development strategy in place, we will not fall into the "shotgun" trap and will always be challenged in a positive way.

Manoeuvre 5: Don't be the "best-kept secret" and make sure to curate your industry credibility and personal brand early.

I grew up in an encouraging and supportive culture where all children irrespective of their gender have an opportunity to flourish. But I also grew up in an Asian culture where humility is greatly valued. As a result, I have never felt truly comfortable in the lime light. One thing I had to learn in the early days of my career was to practise how to accept compliments.

As my career progresses, I made a decision to follow my entrepreneurial spirit and set up my own consulting firm. I loved my decision and have really embraced the freedom and intellectual challenges to undertake a wide variety of projects.

I also quickly learned that to succeed as a small business owner, you cannot be shy or be too humble. While we should not be outrageously boastful, we certainly should consider carefully curating a strategy that draws attention to ourselves in an elegant way. In other words, I had to learn how to curate my industry credibility and personal brand.

Part of being credible is to actually have real relevant experience under your belt, whether it is through formal academic study or life experience. For instance, a significant portion of my professional experience came from the public and non-profit sectors. I realised that I needed to gain some life experience to demonstrate my business acumen. I found my opportunity through chairing an "Innovation and Business Development" sub board committee for a community health organisation that is worth $15 million.

Curating industry authority and personal reputation also involves some savvy media and public relations skills. Learning the language of journalists and ways to discover the best angle to tell my stories were part of my media training journey.

Interestingly, I also had to learn to change my own mind-set when it came to the world of self-promotion. I had to learn to give myself permission to celebrate my success publicly and had to learn to speak about those successful stories to others and to media without feeling self-conscious.

So while being humble is still an important personal belief, I also understand the need to establish my industry credibility and personal brand. After all, it does not matter how good we are, if no one knows about us.

It is, therefore, incredibility important not to fall into the trap of being the "best-kept secret". Make sure to take required steps to build your industry credibility and personal brand in a positive way as early as possible in your career.

As I stood in front of my audience at the United Nations Headquarters in New York City, I thought to myself - *what an unexpected journey this has been.* When I started out many years ago as a medical scientist, I would have never thought one day that I would be visiting the United Nations Headquarters or being part of a team facilitating a global partnership summit.

Life is indeed unpredictable and forever changing, but it also offers endless opportunities for those who are ready to embrace them.

So make sure you are ready.

Suzi Chen

About The Author

Suzi Chen is a cross-disciplinary strategist who manages Notonos Global, an innovation driven business consulting firm that works with clients to "join the dots" and delivers successful business outcomes in an ethical and sustainable manner. The former medical scientist is also an award winning graphic designer, blog contributor and an avid traveler whose journey includes being a summit facilitator at the United National Headquarters in New York City in 2016.

Proud to be an enthusiastic dreamer, Suzi loves the fact that the world is full of possibilities and makes sure she is always challenged by new experiences. This "forward-thinking" mindset is reflected in Suzi's professional career, which spans across a wide range of industries including medical research, emergency management services and non-profit sector. Suzi believes in life-long learning and holds a doctoral degree in medical sciences and several other diplomas. Suzi sits on the company board of 2 non-profit organisations and chairs an Innovation and Business Development committee for a community health service provider.

Email Suzi at shcen@notonos.com. You can follow her on Twitter at @chensuzi or visit www.notonos.com.

Embracing Rosie

Every story starts with a "once upon a time" and finishes with a "happy ever after" and in between the pages there are villains, hero's (in our case heroines), wicked witches, fairies, a few mice and an occasional pumpkin and of course, lost little girls who await the eternal kiss from their Prince Charming.

Rosie Shalhoub's story wasn't always rosy, however it does end in a "happy ever after." She realised the wicked witch was her own critical inner voice, the Fairy Godmother became her "knowing" or as some like to call it her "6th sense" and her Prince Charming came in the form of two very unexpected twins, who were never supposed to have been born and have kept her wide awake ever since. Did we mention her King? He comes later after Rosie saves herself from the damsel in distress she once was, tells the wicked witch where to go and then goes on to save the world.

It was 1967 when Rosie was born, the year dubbed the "Summer of Love" when the Hippie movement was in full swing and the Flower Children were taking over the world. Something must have happened that morning she came into the big wide world, either inhaling too much of the illegal stuff that was floating through the very 60's air or she was reincarnating into a movement of free spirits where she knew she could let her soul run free and wake up 48 years later to find that still the Hippie at heart, this wide eyed girl was about to take the world by storm.

Working in retail ran through her veins as Rosie recalls her very first experiences working in her father's clothing business all but three years old. She would help him put matching shoes back into their boxes, making sure the clothes hangers were all facing the same way and enjoying sitting in the shop window as their very Italian shop merchandiser would turn the windows into something magical. It was no surprise that retail became the very essence of where she built her kingdom and where her love of talking to people started from all those years ago. Where children would be doing whatever children did in the early 70's, Rosie would be down at Shalhoub Bros on Coogee Bay Road talking to strangers and "working" in the family business. A case for child exploitation? Perhaps. However, she grew up learning very valuable skills about business, she learnt how to read different types of personalities and by the time she had grown up she knew how to sell.

After finishing her HSC in 1985 Rosie had no clue what she wanted to do. After taking a course at a secretarial college, which was something you just did back in the 80's, she landed her first real job at AMP. Becoming the personal assistant to the Chief Executive Officer of the department that she can't even remember the name of, Rosie was promoted after only 3 months and was then moved to the stock market department.

She recalls spending time at the stock market, being taking on extravagant lunches, which always turned into dinner, by very wealthy stockbrokers and worked amongst the likes of the then very famous Rene Rivkin, Christopher Skase and Alan Bond.

In 1988 AMP had enrolled Rosie into the Australian Securities Institute where she was trained to be a stockbroker. After achieving high distinctions in all subjects and failing law twice she knew this was not the path her soul yearned for. The fast pace of the city, the long commute and the long hours finally took its toll.

The expensive champagne, the suits and heels and the high salary were swapped for a more laid back lifestyle as she made a complete career move and became an aerobics instructor. Her days were now spent at the gym, her muscles taut and it was here deep in the Sutherland Shire where Cronulla became her home.

In 1993 a freak accident ended her very short lived aerobic career and turned her towards a paint brush. She painted, and she sold. And she sold a lot! Commissions for art work came flooding in.

Rosie fell into a deep depression. Still not knowing what she wanted to do when she grew up. Feeling very unsettled in her then relationship and even more restless within her psyche the needed to find herself and her journey towards enlightenment began. However, somebody forgot to tell Rosie that to become the wise old sage there was going to be a lot of pain, one heck of a journey and a whole heap of synchronicities that the Universe had lined up for her.

Fast forward to 2016 and let Rosie tell you her story for herself...

I still remember that day clearly in 1993 as I was vacuuming my hallway and a small voice in my head said "turn the television on". I was born naturally psychic so voices in my head were a part of the norm for me. However I totally ignored it and kept up with my housework when the voice came back this time louder and clearer "turn on the television".

That was weird for me, as I have never been one to watch much television especially during the day and yet the voice persisted "turn the television on.... turn on the television". Doing what any sane person who thought they were going insane would do I turned on the TV.

Falling to my knees in a heap on the floor I wept to the words of Maryanne Williamson as she spoke to Oprah Winfrey in an interview that not only shook me to the core but changed my world for the rest of my life. Sometimes it's those voices in your head, the feelings in your gut the inner knowing from your inside outs that you just can't ignore. There on the screen in front of me were my two idols Oprah Winfrey and Maryanne Williamson who both became the triggers for where I am today.

At that time in my life I was very miserable. Not content in a marriage I was in and totally broke. I spent days in bed with severe depression. Maryanne's words sank through my veins and I knew that I just had to have her book. The voices in my head weren't just in my head after all. Immediately I rang the local book store to hold a copy of Maryanne's book "A Return to Love" where Oprah reviewed the book and in which Maryanne spoke so clearly about "A Course In Miracles".

I was told the book was on backorder and I had to wait about a week. I then received a phone call 10 minutes later that a copy of the book was available for $3.00. I was at the store within minutes and spent the next two days with my head in the book, studying every single page and getting lost in every single word. From that moment on I became "me" and I knew that I was on a path to help make this world a better place.

My path was clear now in front of me. I was going to work with what came naturally to me, my psychic ability and my creative art. I had no idea at the time that both my natural talents were going to bring me a life that most girls could only dream of.

Lying in bed a week after my Oprah experience I said a prayer. I asked if I was going to save the world then I needed to be shown how. That night I had a dream where a lady came to me, handed me a paint brush and a whole heap of Christmas balls. From then on "Santa's Little Painter's" was born. That very morning I telephoned Westfield Shopping Centre in Miranda and asked to speak to their casual leasing department and I booked a 6 week stand selling hand painted Christmas balls. Everyone thought I had gone nuts.

With a $5000 loan on my credit card, I had no idea what I was doing but I did it anyway. I had spent the past year or so selling my art from market fairs to market fetes, from trade shows to exhibitions. This was during the time when the Internet was still unheard of so my work could only be shown where ever I could take it. I was exhausted, sick of early morning market stalls that would sometimes make me only a few dollars and where people would hustle till they got things for next to nothing. Winter mornings were literally making me sick and I was over it. I was shown a sign in my dream and like the voice in my head I had to go with it.

Westfield was a far cry from the market stands I was used to. This time around I was playing with the big boys, and play I did. With my credit card maxed out I brought $5,000 worth of Christmas baubles. If I had just a dollar for every person who told me I was doing the wrong thing I could have just made my million then and there. Instead of paying a market stall rent of only $60 a day I signed my life away on a lease of $12,000 for a six week period.

Mind you, I had no money to pay this rent. Instead I did a totally Richard Branson thing and worked out how to do it all after I said "yes" and signed on the dotted line. I felt sick, but I had to believe in my gut feelings, my visions, my inner knowingness. Most of all I had to believe in me.

Looking back now as opposed to where Santa's Little Painter's are today, I would say we did look like a market stall that first year, just a higher end one. I painted my little heart out as queues and queues of people waited in line to get the Christmas bauble personalised. I made my 6 week rent in the very first week I operated. Needless to say, I was officially going to be known as the "lady with balls".

Nobody could remove the smile from my face by the time Christmas day came around. Packing up the site late into Christmas Eve I knew I was onto something after estimating a good little profit for myself that year. Let's just say I made in a 6 week period what most people would make in a whole year, all because I followed a dream, and a literal one at that.

My third year into Santa's Little Painter's became the year I learnt my very first lesson in business in making sure all my t's were crossed and my i's dotted. It was also the year I was taught that not everybody is going to be your friend. My year's were filled with clients for psychic readings and they were finished with painting Christmas balls. Life was good, I was making good money and by this stage I had saved enough money to buy myself a gorgeous little bachelorette apartment overlooking the magnificent skyline of the city of Sydney. What was about to unfold however was something that, as a professional psychic, I did not see coming.

I had a wonderful friend who lived in the same apartment block as me. We would spend hours and hours each evening together sometimes over bottles of wine and laugh, and talk and sing and cry. We had a special friendship and I loved her dearly. SLP was in its third year and "A" desperately needed work and money to get her through the Christmas period.

My big heart was excited to have my friend work with me for four weeks and pay her in cash at the end of each day. I was making so much money that I even paid her double what she was entitled to. What harm could that do? Whilst I was helping a friend in need she was counting the dollars in her head.

The week after Christmas had finished "A" asked me if she could go into a business partnership with me. I didn't need a business partner nor did I want one especially one that was such a good friend as I never believed in mixing friends and business. I let her down gently but she was not happy.

I thought it weird that I hadn't heard from her for a week after that very awkward conversation to find a letter addressed to me in the mail from a legal firm. The letter stated that I hadn't paid "A" for a 6 month period she had been working in my establishment (she only worked 4 weeks) and that I had owed her thousands and thousands of dollars. My heart sank, and I thought it was a joke. Knocking on her door I realised when I was asked to leave that this was definitely no joke and I was going to be in big trouble.

Not only did the tax man have his fun with me, the Industrial Relations Court made me feel like the world's biggest criminal. I couldn't understand how this could be as I was the one who was not telling any lies here. I quickly learnt that number one: you don't cheat the tax man and number two: every single business move you make must be put in writing. I fought and fought my case but nothing was going to change as I had done the wrong thing in the first place by paying her cash and not having records to show for it.

The case cost me a lot of money and my solicitor insisted I pay her out on a financial decision as fighting it all the way through the court systems was going to cost me a lot more. Lesson number three: never, ever let your emotions get in the way of making a business and economical decision. I didn't take my own advice though as I wanted to prove I was right. $30,000 later in legal expenses, I don't want to even remember how much was paid out to "A". I was deflated, gutted and totally defeated.

I went away for a long time, a very long time after that experience. I couldn't face the world, it was too harsh a place and the Mediterranean was calling me. Three years later I gave birth to twins, Eliane (pronoucned Elly-Arne) and Joseph. A year after that, I became a single mother, of one year old twins. Life was presenting itself as a big challenge with two little babies, no financial support and only Christmas to get me through. I was too proud to tell my family and friends of the dire straits I was actually in so there was only one thing I could do.

After I fell to a heap on the floor in my lounge room I got back up like the Phoenix from the ashes and gave SLP all I had. Retail runs through my veins so I knew how to sell, and my art came so naturally and easy to me. I was going to franchise my business. Once again, knowing nothing about franchising I found myself sitting in the office of a well known local accountant who specialised in setting up franchise businesses. Not even baby twins, still in their prams and still breast feeding was going to stop me.

I would take the twins to every single meeting I had and if I had to feed them then and there I did. I remember one time at a Westfield meeting I was so unorganised in getting ready to be there on time I threw my jacket on, the babies in the pram and off we walked. I sat down at the meeting to take my jacket off and there in all my glory I had forgotten to put my shirt on! Yes, just me and my very unsexy breast feeding bra in the middle of a busy cafe and very hungry babies.

Back in the accountant's office the accountant thought my idea of franchising was so brilliant that he even had his wife come and sit in on the meetings. We set up the very first SLP franchise in Rhodes shopping centre and here I was starting all over again. Life was good until that following January.

I was asked to have dinner at my accountant's home with him and his wife and I was convinced that we were going to talk about taking over the world with Christmas balls and having Santa's Little Painter's a generic name. History however, was about to repeat itself and instead I was told that the whole franchise business was not a good idea and had no legs to stand on.

You can imagine my surprise when I found out the following Christmas that my franchise idea had been stolen by my accountant. Yes, you read this right. His wife had set herself up in that many shopping centres, there were too many to count. What was the Universe trying to tell me? My ideas, my designs and my whole concept had just been stolen.

Who could I report this to? How could they? Didn't attending meetings with my babies in a pram mean anything to these greedy people? Obviously not. I couldn't report them to anyone, because even though he was an accountant he was also a solicitor and I was very, very, broke, financially and emotionally.

I realised that I must be doing something right if everywhere I turned somebody was trying to take a piece of it from me. They say that the best revenge is success and I used my anger as a fuel, my passion as my motivation and my twins as my driving force. I had lost everything and the apartment that I fought so hard to keep had to go up for sale. My heart was broken and I finally wasn't too proud to ask for help.

You do what you need to do in moments like these even if that meant waitressing. Whilst I waited on tables I had no choice but to turn my lemons into lemonade and I began to actually enjoy the job.

Being the social butterfly that I am I made new friends, became familiar with the regular customers and got to put myself in front of some very high profile people. In case you are wondering where my babies fit into all of this, I have two very amazing parents who stepped in to allow me to do what needed to be done. There are some parts of this story where luck played its role and I am lucky to have the parents I do.

I would have fun with my customers and most of them knew me as the lady with balls or the psychic and some knew me as both. I worked my butt off, I came home to my twins and I planned my following Christmas that I knew was never going to happen as the debt I had accumulated was never going to get me off my feet.

On a chance trip to the bathroom one working day I stopped by to have a chat with my mate Abraham, the owner and brilliant businessman of the Fone King Empire. There were some days I would make myself go the bathroom just so I can have a chat with him and our usual laugh. This day however was different, I was low and sad, I cried in his arms when he asked me how my Christmas planning was going. In all his glory, Abraham became my fairy godfather and before I could blink we became business partners.

Some 13 shopping centres later and Rosie was back! I did what I did best and Abraham did what he did best and together we were a dynamic team. We had a great three years together until once again life was to take both of us in very different directions. Both Abraham and I were presented opportunities that meant we had to kiss each other goodbye and walk down our own yellow brick roads.

I am proud to this day to call Abraham one of my best friends and the most successful and smartest person I have ever met. Whenever I walk past yet another one of his many stores I smile. We finished our last Christmas together with a bang and with Westfield approaching me with an offer I just couldn't refuse. Those days of waitressing paid off, getting to know the managers, staying friendly and grounded and making sure I had my face in front of all the right people. I was offered a shop.

Not only was a shop offered to me, I once again said "yes" without having any idea where the money was going to come from or how as a single mother I was going to pull this off. I signed the lease. I had proven myself with the reputation I had earned with SLP, and I wowed the managers with psychic predictions that always came true. Funny that sometimes my natural talent would at times became my party trick when I needed it to. I knew that life is a game and I had no choice but to play the game well.

The first six months of Embrace's creation we had turned over a whopping 6 figure number. And moving forward six years Embrace has now become the leading provider of spiritual and new age products and the most popular place to go for psychic readings and crystals.

We have had two television shows filmed in our store, celebrities from all over the world come to visit us and we have hosted some of the biggest names in our industry. I am regularly interviewed on radio and I have been interviewed and asked to write an article for the Huffington Post. Before long I had become a public figure and I didn't even know. People come from all over Sydney to visit Embrace as it has now become the hub of the spiritual world.

Going back six years upon signing my lease, the accounts manager at Westfield was very much into the whole spiritual/psychic thing and asked me if I would run a festival for Westfield in line with the whole mind, body, spirit theme.

I had no event training and I had no idea of even where to start. This really wasn't part of the plan and I had no intention of running events, however, without wanting to disappoint and really wanting to make an impression with the managers I once again said "yes". That "yes" word was to become my saving grace for with every "yes" I had to learn and grow a new skill. So, in 2010 we put on our first Embrace Spirit and Wellbeing Festival.

Featured on television and with Westfield backing us, the festival went off with a hit three years running. In 2013 however, we hit a huge fork in the road when Westfield went into major renovations and the Embrace festival had to be put on hold. Or did it? A year into meeting the love of my life, Ross insisted I run the festival out of the Sutherland Shire.

God forbid a girl from the Shire actually leaves the Shire. But now he was suggesting I run my business out of the Shire too! So off he dragged me on an excursion day out to look at venues. Luna Park? No! Technology Park? No! The Hordern Pavilion? We opened the door and there in front of my very psychic eyes I saw the whole festival flash before me. "Yes" became that word again and this time I was really out of my depth.

So I had 9 months to put on a festival and this time around I really didn't know what I was doing. I knew if I could create a pigeon pair of twins in a 9 month timeframe then I could do anything. Every cent I had went into the Festival Of Dreams including the children's pocket money and I felt sick. My vision showed me the festival in full swing so I couldn't be wrong but my gut felt sick so maybe I was wrong. The feelings of anxiety out grew me and I got very sick. For the first time in my life I didn't trust myself and I was truly scared.

What made things worse for me in 2014 was that to pull off an event, like we were about to do, was something that huge corporate teams do. Our team was Ross the builder and I, the lady with balls! If ever I was going to need some balls it was going to be now. So, I did what every girl does in times of crisis - I rang my best friend. Harry known as Harry T (the celebrity psychic medium) and I go back a long way and that is another story for another day.

Harry my very gay BFF always knew how to cheer me up and cheer me up he did. Sometimes it's not always what you know but who you know. And before my very eyes we had Lisa Williams the world's most famous Psychic Medium with her very own reality TV show signing the dotted line on what was about to become Sydney's most talked about spiritual, health and wellness event.

If I thought I had felt sick before, I felt even sicker now. How was I going to not only run Embrace, be a mum of what is now a family of six children 2 my own and 4 Ross's (now that is definitely another story for another day) and pull off a 2 month period of Christmas balls?   It's funny what the human spirit can achieve when your heart and soul is truly in it and when your destiny aligns itself on the right path. I don't think I had ever worked so hard in my whole life. Selling exhibit booths was not as easy as I thought it would be, but now having the divine Ms Lisa Williams name to throw into the selling spiel put us on a whole new level.

People sometimes ask me why I chose the Hordern Pavilion as our venue for the Festival Of Dreams. My answer is always the same, as I wanted an event that was high class, totally and uniquely boutique and somewhere in my thinking I knew that the Hordern would give us instant credibility. It would have been a whole lot easier if we hired a much cheaper venue or even a local RSL venue space but I wasn't going to have it. Embrace is high class and my festival was going to be the same too.

The FOD (Festival Of Dreams) team came together easy once we had signed our contracts - Ross, myself, Adriana and Dianne. (We started with 4 and now there are 8). Days and nights on end we would sit around the kitchen table with children running under our feet, in between soccer and gymnastic training, cooking dinner whilst trying to sound extra professional to potential exhibitors, folding washing as I would dictate emails and running Embrace was truly a year I would never forget. The Festival Of Dreams doors officially opened on 23 August 2014.

Thousands upon thousands of people entered those doors and the media coverage was enormous. Studio10, Sunrise, The Sydney Morning Herald, buses, taxis, posters, we were everywhere! It was almost a bit of a cliché from the movie "Field of Dreams" when the "voice" (the voice I know all so well) would repeat over and over "If you build it they will come". Came they did and Sydney talked.

Our emails were flooded the following week with new potential exhibitors wanting to come on board. We had Hollywood contacting us offering celebrities to attend FOD and I found myself one day totally naked in my shower and laughing out so loud to myself I could have sworn it was all a dream. We didn't call it the Festival Of Dreams for nothing, but the fact that I had finally created my own dream was proving itself a little hard to believe and so I pinched myself to make sure I was still awake.

I was being interviewed on Hollywood radio stations, talking to big US producers over Skype and mixing with movie stars. And so it happened that the 2015 Festival Of Dreams became a Native American theme with Rick Mora and Elder Saginaw Grant. Talk about 6 degrees of separation.

Rick featured in the blockbuster movie Twilight and Saginaw in movies such as the Lone Ranger with Johnny Depp. It was very easy to sell tickets for FOD that year and the once single mother who waited on tables smiled back at me with so much pride that I had to pinch myself again.

Not long after the 2015 FOD I was chatting to a very good friend, well known author and publisher Scott Alexander King from Animal Dreaming Publishing. I have enjoyed reading Scott's work in the past and I like his writing style. Over a very casual conversation one evening I told Scott that I would love to write a book but I have no idea what I would write about.

Scott said that it was easy as you just have to write about something you love. Me being the smarty pants that I always am said "chocolate- I love chocolate, I bet you can't write about that?". Scott proved me very wrong. A year later and "The Chocolate Lover's Message Cards" did not only go to sell in the European market but an American distributor picked them up and they are now selling across the United States.

All of the sudden I became an International author and I proved Oprah Winfrey right - do something you love and the money will follow. Mind you, my body didn't love me for it but it paid off. We are working on some other big projects at the moment but for now that can wait until after Christmas.

Just in case you're wondering where Embrace fits into all of this since the birth of the Festival Of Dreams, stay tuned to your television screen. "Embracing Rosie" the very first reality show to be based on psychics and spirituality has just had its first season of filming and something tells me that I will be joining my chocolate cards in America very soon in the near future.

The past 12 months has proven itself to be the most exciting in my business career as my overnight success had only taken me 25 years to get here. Santa's Little Painter's is back in the franchise game with every Westfield shopping centre being worked on over the next 5 years. The Festival Of Dreams has become a whole new entity itself taking on its own life that has been filled with magic and awe and even Richard Branson himself has become a fan since his chance meeting with our Native American guests last year.

I believe the secret to my success has been a combination of a lot of things starting with the ultimate belief in myself, in my intuition and in my dreams when everyone else had thought I had gone crazy. If I was to ever give advice to anyone who has had to endure the Tall Poppy Syndrome then I would tell them the same thing I have had to tell myself - concentrate on your own business and never ever be afraid of competition as your competitor will only make you greater than you already are.

I have learnt over the years to ask for help when I needed it and I have even learnt to delegate, which was something I found so difficult to do back in the early days. The busier I am the less work I seem to do these days. Making sure you document everything is advice I would always give and that way there is no room for miscommunication.

Always remember your roots and where you came from and always stay humble and grounded. I believe it is important to remember that it is the "little guys" that will make you big and, in the case of retail, it is your regular customers that only need to spend a little with you each week that keep you still standing.

These are the clients that deserve your extra love and care and they surely get it when they walk into Embrace. Remember to always stay in the moment and allow the Universe to conspire to allow all the synchronicities into your life.

I am a firm believer in giving back. FOD works with a charity called Our Big Kitchen in conjunction with Youth of the Streets and Embrace proudly supports the "Free the Bear Foundation". There is nothing more amazing than the feeling of being able to give to another without anything being returned. Financial freedom allows you that and it is in the knowing that another life is being helped because of you.

My career has just been one coincidence after another but it was what I chose to do with those moments that took me from one success to another. Most of all, remember to stay in gratitude, be thankful and grateful for every sale that goes through your cash register. I have not known a sale where I didn't say a silent "thank you", even if it was only for $4.95.

I am grateful when I pay huge tax bills and I say "thank you" because it means that I am making money. I say "thank you" when I pay my staff their wages because without them I wouldn't be where I am today. These are my girls, my "kids" that I like to sometimes call them, my sista's, my friends and my colleagues.

The ones who believe in my dreams as much as I do and I dedicate this chapter to Kati-Rose. Kati was only 14 when she came to work for me, school uniform intact and now 10 years later at 24 I have had the wonder of watching her turn into a beautiful young lady who has become not only my PA, but my babysitter, my nanny and a big sister to my children.

The Festival Of Dreams can be found at www.festivalofdreams.com.au

Embrace can be found at www.embraceaustralia.com.au. Just send us an email, tell me what you thought of my story and how you feel it will help you on your path to success and I will send you an autographed copy of the "Chocolate Lover's Message Cards".

Until next time don't forget to Embrace... Life, Love and Each Other!

Love Rosie xx

Rosie Shalhoub

About The Author

The girl with a big heart and a massive vision! Rosie, the founder of Embrace, was given a vision at a very young age. She always knew that it was part of her destiny to create an environment of love, peace, harmony and beauty that would be shared by many. Although still stuck in a time warp of the 80's, Rosie has always blamed "it" on the gypsy in her soul. A free spirit with a sense of adventure and an attitude for fun, her style has always been quirky & cheeky mixed in with a whole lot of passion & love. Rosie comes from a place of authenticity, courage and wisdom. A true believer in the sacred feminine, with the roar of a warrioress, she is a hopeless romantic, living in a world of make believe, fantasy, humour & love.

Embrace is that world. Embrace's success has a lot to do with Rosie's down to earth attitude and easy approach style. Her background in paranormal psychology, her strong 6 sense combined with her passion, grace and psychic awareness gave way to the birth of Embrace. Embrace is a place of beauty and wonder, Spiritual awareness, love and peace. Rosie's main aim was to bring people together through all walks of life as equals. Through humour, joy and laughter she has managed to do this beautifully, creatively and exquisitely.

Rosie is also the founder/CEO of the Festival Of Dreams, a three day event where you can live your dream life. In her words "The Festival of Dreams is a chance to take time out for yourself and embrace new opportunities to be the best person you can possibly be. At the festival you can make yourself a priority in a judgement free zone and work on your own wellbeing, personal understanding and from that, determine to become the best you can be and live your dream life".

Sometimes dubbed as the "lady with balls", Rosie is also the founder of "Santa's Little Painter's" a thriving business specialising in personalised Christmas baubles.

Rosie lives in Sydney with her partner Ross and her twins Joey and Ellie. She is a mother, lover, daughter, sister, friend, entrepreneur, teacher, writer, author, visionary, dreamer and believer.

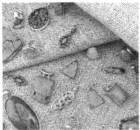

From Nurse to Holistic Skin Specialist

"Your purpose in life is to find your purpose"

Gautama Buddha

As I loitered next to the oxygen cylinders a voice inside my head was calling out with increasing urgency: "Leave. Get out. Get out now."

I had been working on the surgical ward at Bromley Hospital in the South East of England for a couple of years, and this had been a particularly busy and stressful shift. Added into the mix, the nursing manager I was working with had disappeared for a cigarette over an hour ago and still hadn't returned. This was when mobiles had just been born, so there were still only a few people who owned one. The next thing I knew, there was my nursing colleague and superior, being wheeled onto the ward in a hospital bed – she had gone for a fag and then admitted herself with suspected appendicitis, leaving me in charge of twenty-six very sick patients, and fuelling my secret suspicion that she had a case of the Munchausen's. (Needless to say her appendix was perfectly healthy).

That was it! This was the final push I needed to finally leave the NHS behind to pursue something alternative. I was fed up with being taken for granted, left in the lurch and told what to do, so knew I wanted to work for myself, but doing what? This was the olden days, when connecting to the Internet meant plugging a wire into the wall and listening to a strange extra-terrestrial dialling tone before Yahoo popped up on your screen. I spent hours researching possible career avenues, and soon realised that I had a real interest in alternative approaches to health.

By this time I had a young baby, so knew whatever I chose had to fit in with being a mum. When someone lent me a book about essential oils, I was enraptured and soon began experimenting on my family and around the home with different oils. The use of aromatics for healing purposes has been traced back to ancient Egypt, around 3500 BC. I was particularly interested in the fact that massaging different types of essential oils into the face and neck can bring about powerful responses in our skin. For example, many of us know that Tea Tree has antibacterial benefit, but I also learned that lesser known oils such as Fennel, Clary Sage and Wild Thyme are equally antiseptic.

Essential oils - like many modern women - are multi-tasking, as their scents also have clinically proven benefits to the mind. Coming from a scientific background, I am always keen to ensure that these aromatherapy-type claims have clinical research to back them up, and I am never disappointed. For example, a trial involving 79 college students with sleep disorders reported better sleep patterns and awaking feeling refreshed after just 5 nights of inhaling Lavender essential oil(*). In addition, the benefits were still going strong two weeks post-trial when the subjects were followed up. Another study proved that inhaling Ginger essential oil during chemotherapy treatment significantly reduces nausea and vomiting, and improves appetite**.

In terms of skincare, numerous trials have looked at the benefit of essential oil application to adult and child eczema, dermatitis and dry skin. One such trial showed that a blend of Lavender and Tea Tree oils had an immediate effect by soothing itching***, and several studies carried out on Rose, Helichrysum and Bergamot essential oils have highlighted that these botanical extracts have powerful antioxidant benefit, meaning that they are able to protect our skin from free radicals. ****

Completely sold on the supreme benefit this therapy could impart to my future customers, I enrolled on a Clinical Aromatherapy course. This qualification meant I could eventually help people sort out the root cause of their health issues, rather than just the symptoms. I decided to do an extra module to learn how essential oils can be used to exert their unique benefits onto skin, both through direct application as well as inhaling their scents.

From the moment I started my course in London, I absolutely loved it – this felt so right and I was immediately fascinated – still am - by the power and benefit of essential oils; truly a gift from nature. I clearly remember my first day when I made a simple blend of Lavender and Patchouli, and a fellow classmate massaged it into my shoulders. I felt heady, completely relaxed and I was hooked. The great thing with scents is that they jog memories, and I am always transported back to that day every time I work with these specific essential oils.

I met a lovely lady on the course, Sara, and by the time we'd qualified, had decided to team up to help each other out. Sara had an existing client base because she owned a clinic and she began referring her clients to me, and vice versa. This became the first lesson I learned about business: three to the power of two – meaning, there is true strength in collaborating with others of similar mind sets, in helping each other and creating a strong story together.

It was 2000 and very quickly I had a small group of clients I was working closely with on various health issues, yet they all had one thing in common – imbalanced skin. Some of the imbalances seemed insignificant on the surface in that they were easy to treat – dryness or dehydration for example – but I became aware that I could only do so much healing through the use of essential oils and Aromatherapy alone. As I delved deeper into the realms of these clients' lifestyles, I realised that stress, poor diet and sleep patterns (to name a few), also play a huge role in our skin's condition and wellbeing.

Enter business lesson number two: adapting to your client's needs equals wonderful customer service. If you do something new for your clients, they feel special, and they are more likely to remain loyal, (plus it makes you feel all fuzzy inside). So, I decided to add to my skill set by doing a course in Skin Nutrition – how to nourish skin from the inside out through diet and care of the gut. I developed the practice of promoting good gut circulation alongside a realistic dietary routine for my clients, because so many people have poor gut absorption, meaning they gain zero benefit from eating the right foods, however many supplements they take or platefuls of kale they might consume.

I also began making bespoke skincare for my customers at this point – natural, organic facial oils, creams and balms designed and tailor-made for their skin and mind. They could even select a preferred type of scent – whether they preferred woody, fresh, calming or floral base notes. Often I would infuse products with raw juice from herbs and flowers such as parsley, sage and tamarind, or tea extracts such as Rose Hip and Fennel to make the skincare as fresh as possible, and I was literally making everything from home on the work surfaces in my kitchen, frequently at night once the children were in bed.

This led to my third and fourth business lessons: create a niche for yourself in a crowded market and let your work speak for itself. There were lots of other Clinical Aromatherapists around at the time, but I was coming from a fresh angle. My clients were happy, and word was spreading. I was also formulating tailor-made blends for the body; one client had lymphatic oedema in her right arm following a right mastectomy. She was very self-conscious of her swollen arm, felt that people were staring at her when she was in company and that it was a tell-tale sign of her former illness.

I had cared for lots of mastectomy patients as a nurse, and knew this was a very common problem following breast surgery as there are some great, whopping lymphatic drainage ducts in the upper body, which become imbalanced through the surgery, meaning that drainage becomes difficult. For this lady, I suggested a combination of regular lymphatic drainage massage and an essential oil blend to promote good blood flow through her arm, shoulders and thorax (chest). I chose Geranium, Oregano, Rosemary and Lemon, which all work to encourage blood flow in the body and so oxygen supply to the tissues. These are also naturally detoxifying, cleansing oils to purify skin and blood, which smell gorgeous and have a similar boosting effect on the mind.

The lady came to see me once weekly and we used her oil to massage over these areas, plus she continued this at home three more times every week. The results were astounding - she was wearing short sleeves again within a month and crucially, her confidence and self-esteem soared.

I also had many male clients with all sorts of skin issues. I recall the first time I saw one gentleman in particular who originally came to see me about his adult acne; well actually, he had suffered with back acne since he was a teenager but he now had cystic acne to the mid and lower face. When I see a client for the first time, I am often assessing them for what they are *not* saying; subtle body movements for instance, how they dress, their posture, and so on. This was a leftover nursing skill, picked up through years of reviewing new patients. The man was dressed entirely in black. It was a sunny day and he wore a hat with a huge brim pulled down over his eyes. He also covered his mouth a lot when he spoke. In short, I could see that he was agonisingly self-conscious about his skin, and it was dramatically affecting his everyday life.

I developed a programme for him, providing him with recipes to make his own daily face masks at home using edible ingredients, (giving him autonomy over his treatment), whilst making him a range of bespoke skincare products containing raw, natural and organic extracts, plus weekly aromatherapy treatments. I also referred him for stomach acid assessment and designed a dietary programme, including foods high in antioxidants and low in wheat, dairy and GM ingredients. I advised him to swap all of his household cleaning, shaving products and fragrance for plant-based ones. The products I made for him were designed to balance his skin and uplift his spirit, and included an essential oil blend of Sweet Orange, Chamomile, Ledum and Sandalwood to support the nervous system and liver. He was able to burn the blends around the home, as well as apply to his pulse points throughout the day. His acne quickly changed to a non-inflammatory form and he was delighted. I worked closely with this client over many years and he has become a close friend.

After 5 or so years, I had a waiting list of clients. I had three children by now and wasn't always able to meet demand. Sometimes I drove out to clients' homes to see them in the evenings, which was hard when I might not have slept much the night before, or if one of the boys was poorly, but my passion for and belief in my business always spurred me on. In 2012 my business was 12 years old, and I was seeing clients from all over the UK and Europe too. Until now, much of my work had been 'underground' – I hadn't invested in exotic advertising or PR, relying on word of mouth only. I felt ready to take the business to the next level and the first thing I decided to do was set up a proper skincare brand, based on blends I had used with my clients, who provided me with an existing customer base.

Although I was able to use the lessons I had learned from the Aromatherapy business, I soon realised this was a slightly different ball game.

Skincare is what I would describe as fiddly – packaging design, labelling, the product inside and the presentation must all come together beautifully and quite often, even with the best intentions, it simply doesn't work so you have to scrap everything and start over. I remember spending an entire Sunday evening trying to put a new roll of labels onto some glass bottles I had invested in. Each time I applied one, unsightly bubbles would form over the surface and the labels would crease up. After a few hours of approaching this supposedly simple task through many different methods, I was so hot, frustrated and close to tears that I had to admit defeat. I later learned that this was because the labels were made out of paper, which is always difficult to apply.

During an early London launch of the skincare business, my PR lady had to stop me from unpacking boxes of products in front of the journalists; I was so used to being hands-on I didn't realise that this was not the done thing within the world of beauty. And of course the thought of speaking to the editors and bloggers present made me quiver, but I reminded myself to be authentic and allow my passion for my business to come through. On several occasions I dispatched orders to clients, who then e-mailed me to tell me something had leaked or everything was smashed when it arrived, so I would have to spend time re-making the products and dispatching them all over again. Yes, getting the skincare brand, which I named Inner-Soul Organics - off the ground took a lot of mental strength on a daily basis, and I had to watch where every penny went like a hawk, as I was self-funding.

To save on costs, I built my own website initially which took me a total of nine months, and sourced packaging and ingredients in small quantities. I also formulated everything myself and found an independent chemist's apprentice to do all the product safety testing. My brilliant designer Mike, and London-based manufacturer, Steve, helped to make it all a lot smoother and I launched a small range for face, bath and body in the August of 2012, all created using fresh, organic plant extracts.

The global skincare market was worth around 96 billion USD in 2012, and today has grown to 121 billion USD, so it was of utmost importance that I stuck to my business lesson number three, creating something to set me apart from other skincare brands. Inner-Soul Organics products are made in small batches, often fresh to order, using raw, antioxidant extracts with proven skin benefit.

The brand today offers seventeen products across face, bath and body, plus unisex, Mum and Baby, Nordic-Inspired and Bespoke options, and won its first skincare award within the first few months of trading. I have employed a lovely part-time publicist in-house and the brand appears regularly in respectable press, plus I contribute to various magazines, including The

Peridot Mag and www.getthegloss.com. We have won several more awards in spite of being a small company, and this past year have tripled our turnover.

This process has taught me my fifth business lesson: stay focused on what you believe in. It sounds obvious, maybe a little cheesy, but I have often repeated this mantra to myself over the years, especially when things get tricky. I sometimes imagine I'm on a path, and look at what is at the end of the path for my current business goal, which might be a product launch or a new supplier. If I want something, I visualise myself having it, and implicitly trust my own judgment. I also try to treat others how I wish to be treated and never promise to deliver something I can't.

My career journey has taken me from the vocational to the commercial and it's been a huge learning curve. But at night when it's quiet, I still think about those oxygen cylinders and how they led me to build a fulfilling and fascinating business, which I dearly love.

Emma Coleman

REFERENCES:

*Effect of Inhaled Lavender and Sleep Hygiene on Self-Reported Sleep Issues: A Randomized Controlled Trial. Lillehei AS et al

** Effects of inhaled ginger aromatherapy on chemotherapy-induced nausea and vomiting and health-related quality of life in women with breast cancer. Lua PL et al

*** Case History of Infected Eczema Treated with Essential Oils, C. Blamey et al

**** Biological properties and resistance reversal effect of Helichrysum italicum (Roth) G. Don E. Guinoiseau et al; Antioxidant Activities and Volatile Constituents of Various Essential Oils, Alfreda Wei and Takayuki Shibamoto

About The Author

Emma started off as a nurse (NHS) in the 90's before qualifying as a Clinical Aromatherapist in 2000 specialising in her passion, care of the skin. After subsequently taking a course in Skin Nutrition, she worked closely with clients, creating tailor-made programmes to balance their various skin issues with a unique, holistic approach through education, and tailor-made natural and organic skincare routines and dietary input.

Her services grew through word of mouth as the results were so visual, she launched her own skincare brand Inner-Soul Organics – available at www.inner-soul.co.uk - in 2012 using raw, antioxidant ingredients to protect and nourish skin. Emma still formulates and designs every product in the award-winning ranges today and continues to work with a few clients and their families throughout the UK and Europe.

Emma says, "As well as loving the process of designing and creating products and holistic skin programmes, I passionately believe each skin type is individual to us and factors such as lifestyle, natural sleep pattern, diet and personality must be considered. Therefore, each of my clients is viewed as unique – one-size-fits-all simply doesn't work in sorting out skin issues."

Many of the products in the Inner-Soul Organics range are based on tailor-made skincare designed for Emma's former clients; for example Circulation Boost Skin Oil is based on a massage product originally formulated for a lady who, following a mastectomy, had developed Lymphoedema to her left arm.

Inner-Soul Organics offers freshly made skincare products from anti-ageing, unisex to pregnancy-friendly, plus individually created bespoke products.

E-mail: emma@inner-soul.co.uk

Instagram: InnerSoulOrganicsSkincare

Facebook: InnerSoulOrganics

Twitter: @EmmaInnerSoul

YouTube: InnerSoulOrganicsTV

Building More Than Just a Salon

Hairdressing was not ultimately what I wanted to do as a career, when I was at school I first wanted to be a ballerina. I eventually grew out of that notion and my ambition switched to being accepted at Glasgow School of Art. Whilst studying I applied for a Saturday job for a salon group called Irvine Rusk, who at that time had a growing reputation in Glasgow for being an up and coming name in hairdressing.

A friend informed me that I would have to be able to shampoo hair and would possibly be asked to demonstrate this at my interview. I practiced on anyone that would let me try for a week before and was hugely disappointed that this was not part of a Saturday girl interviewing process.

I just loved the job, dealing with the public and being creative at the same time. What really appealed to me was the glamorous side to our industry, as Irvine Rusk were part of a new generation that were producing creative photographic work, taking part in shows and seminars and working as platform artists on stage. Scottish hairdressing was gaining a reputation for being one of the best in the world, this combined with an awareness of current clothes fashion, art and interior design.

It appealed to both the artist and ballerina inside me, so I decided then and there that this was the career choice for me. I did not return to school and started my full time training and at sixteen I knew I would one day have my own business.

In 1982 I took the opportunity to change job and started working with Alan Stewart (now my husband), who had opened a 2,500 square foot salon in the heart of Glasgow's city centre. He had previously been a partner/art director with Irvine but had decided to follow his own destiny. He had a strong vision of how he would like a salon environment to be and the type of company he would like to run.

The salon was quite radical to all other salons in Glasgow, one because of its size but also his concept of giving clients a bespoke service, longer appointment times, in-depth consultations, luxury products, advanced colouring techniques and charging premium prices. He also was very involved in education, hair shows, seminars producing photographic work for magazines and he was looking for an artistic team to work alongside him.

I then had the opportunity to explore the creative side in me and loved creating avant-garde hair for shows, learning how to style hair for photographs, innovating new haircutting, colour and perming techniques and demonstrating them either on stage or in the classroom. This totally consumed me. We would work for nine hours in the salon working on our clients then would practice at night on models, wigs, concepts, and we even hired a tutor to help us with public speaking, videoing ourselves on stage then critiquing our performance. We had very limited resources then, so my dancing experience was put to good use choreographing presentations and Alan and I learned how to apply make up for stage and camera.

I also became the PR for the salon and wrote press releases and mailed out information and photographs to all the UK and international hair publications. We also produced a series of 20 educational video tapes based on our cutting techniques. All of this effort started to pay off, as we were in demand to perform in the USA, Australia, South Africa and Europe and took part in major trade events in the UK. It sounds very glamorous but we were still on very limited budgets, when we were demonstrating at the London trade shows, both the team and the models accompanying us travelled down on public transport (overnight bus) sometimes without even a seat, and I would have made packed lunches for all.

We often had groups of foreign students coming to Glasgow to learn from us, and we needed more space to be able to facilitate the education arm of the business, so an opportunity arose in 1984 to buy a salon that was prime site, a couple of hundred yards from the flagship salon.

This was a salon that Alan had previously managed for another company, and he had made it a huge success in its time but now the owners wanted to retire. Alan opened this opportunity up to the art directors working for him, and wanted a commitment and large deposit to make one of us a partner in the business. The new salon would be predominantly a hairdressing education facility with a small salon attached. This was the opportunity I was looking for and the next day I put my flat on the market to raise the capital.

We had major plans for the space, which included the latest interior design, which did not come cheap. We also had a substantial bank loan to fund the project. Having your own business is a steep learning curve, I was having to learn a new set of skills as we did not have the resources to employ a team. My duties included, opening and closing the salon, cashing up daily, writing hand financial and stylist trend reports, bookkeeping, paying wages on Kalamazoo weekly,(this also entailed going to the bank and getting the exact cash amounts to put in envelopes) filing VAT returns, stock procurement, ordering/taking, daily management/running the business, dealing with quality control, hiring and firing, training the team, running an advanced training academy, bookings, course planning and teaching. Now we have a team, and work with agencies that specialise in their field, but the beauty of starting off so lean, and developing the business as a team, is that there is not a job that someone does for us now that we do not know how to do or have done.

We were quite naïve then and did not have a plan B, if we did not fill our school up every week with foreign students. We thought "if you build it, they will come". Our jolly bank manager changed and Alan and I received a call from our new bank manager who forcibly pointed out that we were spending more weekly than we were bringing in. We were continuing to travel the world and not really getting paid enough for the time effort and money we were spending pursuing this avenue, coupled with not enough students and a small hairdressing staff. He told us it all had to change, with immediate effect and if we did not bring in more money this week he would not pay the staffs wages. This was the biggest wakeup call we ever got. We honestly thought we were going to lose not just one salon but both salons and if he were to decide to retract the loan we would also lose our homes. We had been working as hard as we could with the ultimate goal to create a reputation for producing and teaching the best in our craft, and making money was the last thing on our agenda.

We did not go to bed that night and poured over the figures, how could we save money and how could we increase our turnover. The figures kept coming back with the same sum, we would have to double our turnover/number of clients and number of staff within a week. This was just not possible, then we looked at it from a different angle it was the profit we needed not the turnover, so a plan was hatched, we would sell two day seminars to all the local salons, and do these on a Sunday and Monday, we enlisted a local rep from a salon suppliers and paid him a commission on every seminar he sold. We had worked out if we could get ten people per two days, for a few weeks this would give us the reprieve we needed. Then we could work on increasing the salon staff and clientele.

It was a shock to us that this rep came back and said he has sold sixty tickets and could we give him more dates as he could sell the same again. We also at that time abandoned the idea of an advanced Academy and focused on training our own people. It took us eighteen months to completely turn the business around. We worked seven days a week, as many hours as it took. Not long after we had got everything back on track we received an invitation to the boardroom from the bank manager, to attend a four course lunch to celebrate the success of our business, I can remember whispering to Alan, do you think there is some poor business owner downstairs, being told the bank will not pay their wages?

When we started we were working on a vision and a passion but coming so close to losing everything, I changed my focus and I remember saying to

Alan, I no longer want to be recognised for being the best hairdresser but for being the best business woman in the industry. We then became business junkies, attending business seminars, reading every book we could find, attended motivational courses and at night watched videos relating to business, coaching, and self-development and in the car always had a tape in the cassette. Alan started as my business partner and through our shared vision and passion for learning, we eventually became a couple.

We also took the opportunity to take a major step in 1990 and purchased a 6,000 square foot, five story building on the opposite side of the square from the second salon, we needed more space to educate our growing team and had decided to add beauty to our services. Anyone from the outside looking in would scratch there head as to why we would open three large salons within a few hundred yards from each other? When we opened the second salon, the first did not lose any new business, and through developing people both businesses grew, so we applied the same principal to the third and it was a success. This meant that we dominated the Glasgow city centre market.

With all this newfound knowledge, we implemented structure, systems, ideas, to both our business and team, continually imparting our knowledge on the team. This resulted in our team growing in size, knowledge, ability and nurturing and developing them as both hairdressers and individuals, working on developing their strengths. This then resulted in producing a really strong team who all were like minded and wanted to be part of our growing business who had bought in to our values and culture. I worked on a ten year plan, with education being the mainstay and worked on how we could evolve and how the team could be part of it. We decided to go down the route of franchising the business, this would allow us to benefit but the individual would have the opportunity to be in control of their own income and benefit from the work they put in. We only franchise to our own people, who know and understand the brand and standards. We also developed our own product range to reflect our philosophy on working with the best hair condition. We have a policy for sustainable organic growth in all avenues of the business and have underpinned the business with the property arm and where possible have purchased most of the salon properties.

We have at present twelve salons, making us the largest, both in size and staff numbers salon group in Scotland. Not only have the salons grown but so has the education arm of our business. We eventually opened a standalone school in 2002, but quickly grew out of the space and in 2006 opened a 7,500sq foot state of the art academy in Glasgow. We have won many awards for our education and a recent HMI report gave us four excellent score. We were also filmed for over a year for BBC Scotland and starred in a four part documentary following the career of ten brand new trainees.

We also nurtured a team to work on the artistic side of the business and they continue to show the Rainbow Room International brand of hairdressing and are ambassadors for the company. We have a team who work on events, T in the Park, Baftas, Mobos etc. and have styled many celebrities and stars.

We had many other challenges along the way, our second salon was flooded from the offices above and we did not realise we were under insured and had to use all of our wits to keep the business afloat. We had to manage the situation because it was a listed building, due to the restrictions we had to let it dry our naturally, which took a year. We moved in to the other salon across the road - this did lose us clients and suppressed the growth of both salons during this period. When we bought the building in Royal Exchange Square, even although we had four different types of surveys, when work started, the floors would not take the load capacity and we ended up in the basement looking at the roof.

Our industry is a vibrant creative one and it gives you the opportunity to become anything you want, an artist, teacher, manager, salon owner, but it does take hard work and dedication. I still have a few clients that I like to do their hair. It is the clients that keep the job interesting. They come from many walks of life and have extended knowledge of all subjects. I feel that you have to keep growing, learning and never be afraid to make mistakes or take chances. I always say to our team, unless you are taking calculated risks and pushing forward, the minute you step off the path and just try to hang on to what you have got, then it is a slippery road to going backwards. During the recession of 2008 we stepped up and increased the education of the team, put the focus on taking our service to new levels instead of trying to cut back.

We have succeeded by always trying to be the best, first or different. Sometimes not all of our ideas have worked, but the team expect change, although it is slightly more difficult the bigger we get to turn the whole ship round overnight, but we are always open to new ideas. We have communication on all levels, as head office is in the Academy we see all the trainees on a weekly basis, and the whole team have to attend at least four advanced training courses a year. Alan and I personally run consultation, team building, management and train the trainer courses, throughout the year. We also have senior management meetings every four weeks.

We have our level of success though the synergy of the team work, have management teams, training teams, blog squad, artistic teams, and reception teams, and bring people together to improve systems and quality. Each year, for the past 30 years, we come together for a Staff Congress. The first one was very small, giving out crystal glasses as prizes and a day conference with on overhead projector. It has grown into a full day conference, which guest speakers, hair show and a glittering awards dinner art night. Our pay system factors in annual bonuses and in 2016 we gave out £60,000 in bonus cheques. We have many categories in our personalised RRI awards. The more prestigious awards are given for continual improvement. This is a system we adopted 30 years ago after a visit to Japan, to encourage small continual improvements. The night is always a great testament to the team work of the company, although the salons do compete with each other, they all celebrate each other's achievements.

We are aware that future clients are very different and we have to keep up with technology, we have put a major focus on managing our social media and using a media agency who work closely with our PR agency. It is another skill set that we need to learn, but it is important to keep up with all the technology, we realised that on-line was growing and 18 years ago we commissioned a computer developer to write our own on line booking/ salon management programme. This was again another of life's experiences, the budget started at £30,000. At the time, there was not a live booking systems for clients (book and get an E Mail Back) the first company folded and another company took over and between the two companies it ended up costing ten times original cost.

We have built up a very recognisable brand, and by some we are referred to as an institution. This has been achieved through dedication, hard work and a passion for educating others and ourselves, not being afraid to fail and being innovative.

Linda Stewart

About The Author

Rainbow Room International are Scotland's most successful hairdressing and beauty salon group, with twelve award-winning salons throughout the country they are regarded throughout the global hairdressing industry as leaders and innovators.

Rainbow Room International are passionate about education and already have their very own training academy and fame academy within Glasgow city centre. Their Academy of Hair situated at 64 Howard Street, Glasgow is one of the largest in Europe and confirmed Rainbow Room International as one of Europe's leading hairdressing brands.

With a floor area of 7,500 sq ft dedicated to student development, this state of the art academy of hair has opened the way for candidates throughout the UK, to learn and achieve qualifications such as NVQ 2/3 and

Modern Apprenticeships as students at the forefront of today's most advanced development programme.

As well as being a centre of education for the Rainbow Room International team, the academy is open to non Rainbow Room International staff and attracts many hairdressers from the UK and overseas. The academy has its own inspirational training prospectus of courses running and also acts as a Schwarzkopf centre of education offering Schwarzkopf ASK courses.

Rainbow Room International's Academy of Hair provides highly motivated professional coaches, all of whom gained their knowledge and experience within the renowned Rainbow Room international education and training system. The student learning programme utilises fully integrated video, DVD, and online technologies as part of the theory development, and, in addition to the vast experience available to students through the Rainbow Room International group, students are regularly exposed to motivational demonstrations by the highly acclaimed Rainbow Room International Art Team.

This outstanding facility compliments many years experience in the development of techniques for early student training and beyond to advanced and creative styling techniques.

Rainbow Room had commissioned a gallery of hands from the most creative and motivating hairdressers including Vidal Sassoon, Trevor Sorbie, Annie Humphreys, Tim Hartley and Luis Llongueras.

Rainbow Room International directors Alan and Linda Stewart are extremely proud of Academy of Hair; "The reason behind the opening of the academy was that we needed premises large enough to cope with 100 trainees a day for our company plans. Once we found suitable premises it was down to creating a space that young trainees and hairdressers from across the globe would like to come and work within. It had to be a world class training centre, be easy to manage and have multi-usable spaces/studios that could be changed from lecture theatre style to salon to photographic studio with minimal disruption and as quickly as possible.

Throughout the development of the academy a lot of custom building was required but well worth it to achieve the concept successfully. We did not want to lose the immense feeling of space so we used a considerable amount of glass to keep the open and airy feeling. It also allows our head of training to monitor where everyone is and how courses are progressing at any time during the day.

The academy has already allowed us to work more efficiently and is a fantastic environment to work in. The academy has increased the number of internal and external students learning within Rainbow Room International and we are delighted with the project and the standards that are being achieved."

Rainbow Room International Academy of Hair
64 Howard Street, Glasgow, G1 4EE
Tel: 0141 221 0400
www.rainbowroominternational.com

Beads, Yoga, & Chai! Oh My!

From an early age, I remember diving into creative, entrepreneurial pursuits. Whether it was selling donuts during the neighborhood garage sales or writing poems at age seven to making jewelry for all my friends. By age thirteen, I remember sitting at a dear friend's family kitchen table as we brainstormed how to start a business in homemade lip gloss and make up. The spirit has always been ignited within me. I could attribute it to the hard work ethic of my father or the boldness of my mother. Regardless, beneath my skin runs the blood of a creative servant and it has been the director of my life.

I have learned that things do not come easy and if it comes easy it leaves even easier. There must be a force behind the show that keeps it going. And I realized, as I dreaded working in the restaurant industry and the retail industry, that I did not want to work for 'the man'. I got bored easily and was simply too stubborn. I was going to live my life on my own terms.

However, at the time; it was not some bold pursuit to live on my own terms but a gentle whisper to follow my heart. As a college student, battling manic depression - I found absolute solace in the yoga practice. By month four of a consistent yoga practice I felt different. I knew that these classes, poses, and practices were changing me and healing me in ways that medication and counseling wasn't. It was then that my heart yearned to pass this powerful technology of healing on to others. And so I did.

It was not long before I pursued extensive training in Yoga Therapy and married my high school sweetheart. He had recently returned from a deployment to Afghanistan and inspired me to serve the military demographic through yoga and mindfulness. Having big trust, I closed my eyes dropping out of college and jumped into a new town to serve and do the work I was so passionate about. The truth about starting your own business is that it will go nowhere and you are nobody to everybody unless you do the work, promote your work, and delineate the value you offer. If I don't do it for my company, nobody else will do it for my company. It was my clarity in the direction I wanted to go that wrapped me in the confidence which attracted clients and partnerships paving the path to success.

There is power in partnerships. However, power can be used for both good and bad. The beauty as a business owner is that the bad provides incredible curriculum to grow. You dust your feet off and try again but a little wiser and a little better. Living in Fort Bragg as a new military wife at age 20, it was easy to discount the value and wisdom I could offer to my clients due to my being so young compared to others in the market.

As I found teaching gigs, I continued to look for more opportunities to teach privately in a therapeutic setting. It was serendipity when I connected with Angie Toman, my mentor and colleague. We connected by craigslist, I responded to her ad. Thus leading to an interview conducted at her home as she was putting her groceries away after coming back from the grocery store. We will always laugh at how laid back and unique our circumstances were that brought us together. And she took a chance on me. At the time, I felt so lucky. In reality it was not luck, but preparedness meeting an opportunity.

A proverb teaches that wise men seek council. We can learn so much from our mentors and even more from simply having a humble heart and showing up in our day to day life. Soon after Angie and I met and began working together, she opened up Living Balance Studios where I was able to facilitate Yoga Therapy and manage the business in a contractor position. To be heard and seen, one must put themselves out there.

And that is exactly what I did. I built my clientele through volunteering in the community, attending networking events, and connecting with medical professionals on the military base and in the community. After a couple years of consistent perseverance and the will to serve and teach; I was the youngest professional to ever be named one of Fayetteville's Top 40 Under 40. I was a contributing writer on health and wellness for many local publications, participated on an advisory board to build a facility to support our wounded warriors, and was writing programs and leading retreats to serve our wounded veterans and service men and women.

Creativity is so important to me. I believe that creativity is one of the reasons I love teaching yoga so much. Because each sequence is a creative flow and each class I teach is different. I love designing. I designed and built my website, marketing materials, social media promotions, my home, even my journals are decorated and detailed by design. I live my life by design which partly inspired me to start making jewelry.

It started on a day of self-care with beads and intention. It began as a gift for myself and through compliments and conversation; I began making jewelry for my students, clients, local boutiques and wellness shops, events, and more. What made MelMarie jewelry so unique was the special notes and intentions that I would write on the header cards. Whether it was custom made for an individual or a general piece on display at the studio; the bracelets were an outward reflection of an inward intention.

They served as a reminder for people to stay connected with their affirmations and wellness. Eventually, I couldn't keep up with the orders and made the decision with another one of my mentors to begin sourcing my jewelry.

An obstacle that I had to overcome was an obstacle that faces many; the fear of being judged by others. Because I had made my jewelry handmade for so long, after I switched over to sourcing, one of the individuals who would order bracelets from me commented that she no longer supported it because it wasn't handmade anymore. Even though they were the same designs and had the same love, message, and careful thought infused into it- all the sudden it wasn't good enough.

Although, this was one comment from one person; I began over thinking, which led to self-doubt. Over thinking is the most insidious and devious form of self- sabotage that exists. That is when my jewelry sales slowed down- not because they were sourced but because of my own attitude and insecurities.

One morning, I was wearing one of my bracelet stacks and was admiring it. The bracelets inspired me as I thought about the lesson and affirmation from its header card. It was that morning I realized that I had handed my power over to someone and this made up fearful. It was that morning, I took my power back. I am so proud of my designs and from there, I began to get orders and saw how these bracelets were inspiring those who wore them. The messages were landing and serving- and that is all that mattered.

One of my mantras is a quote by St. Benedict. It goes "Ora Est Labora" meaning my work is my prayer. The only witness to belief is action. It is through our deliberate action that expounds genuine hope and conviction. Furthermore, when we ask, we will receive in some way or form. Angie Toman was an answered prayer as she provided me the space to facilitate my service.

Reflecting on many of my classes and private sessions; I would always be affirmed through the feedback I would receive or the testimonies of healing, wellness promotion, and positive lifestyle changes that my clients would celebrate and share. When someone comes to you, dependent on a cane to walk to her mailbox and within months is no longer using a cane and can balance on one foot. Or someone who hasn't slept a full night in years and has extreme inflammation within the body via rashes and metabolic syndrome, but within weeks is in tearful gratitude that the rashes are clearing up and that the practices are helping them sleep. So many cases, only fueling my passion for yoga therapy and mindfulness.

As I continue to grow my business, one thing that I believe sets me apart is that I serve with a high level of excellence towards my clients. I remember old cartoons with skits about 'The customer is always right!' and as they play satire to our service industries; stressing the idea of putting the customer first is imperative. This is ultimate service. I meet my clients where they are. I hear their needs. And I show up fulfilling what I offer. I keep service and devotion above all other components of my business. Furthermore, I honor my own self-care because a deep truth for me is that you cannot serve from an empty vessel.

Some of my students laugh at how I use words like cozy, grounded, and yummy to describe self-care. In both my work and personal life, I go the extra mile to stay grounded and 'make it cozy'. These are ways I can consistently nourish myself and share the art of self-care and living well to others.

Whether it be my vinte no water soy chai latte that accompanies me to classes or the confidence in saying, "no". These are all sacred practices of self-care that are the foundation of my success. We can only extend to others what we have offered to ourselves. Success, you ask, what is success? Success is achieving joy, contentment, and peace in each moment of your life. To yield quality and be present. To value connection over perfection. When we honor what is truly important to ourselves and abide in it, we have become successful.

When my husband was relocated to Fort Sam in San Antonio to complete his nursing courses in the Army, it was then that I experienced the struggle that I have heard many accounts of other military spouses talk about. Relocating, means starting over. As a military spouse, I understand that nothing is permanent and anything can change in a moment.

At the time, we were under the impression we would be staying in San Antonio for only a year (it ended up being extended to three years). Again, nothing is permanent and anything can change in a moment. I had to rearrange the way my yoga therapy looked due to my resistance in rebuilding a clientele since we were not promised to stay very long. That is when I took another jump and took my business virtual. I got certified in holistic life coaching and began facilitating coaching calls.

Resilience is a common word you hear among the military community. To adapt and rearrange. I am grateful for providence pushing me out of my comfort zone and prompting me to problem solve. To ensure I stay devoted to serve by teaching, I trusted myself and expanded my services. I remember in college, someone once said to me 'ask for forgiveness, not permission'.

Often I would catch myself seeking validation from others in hopes that I would receive permission to go for it or try it or pursue it or post it. One of the biggest obstacles I have overcome in my career and life is giving myself permission to not know all the answers and just go for it. Furthermore, to no longer wait and ask for permission but to wholeheartedly follow the projects and ideas planted in my heart.

Because of this principle, I am the coauthor with Dr. Kyle Hoedebecke of *The Innate Design: Implementing Self-Healing Techniques for the Modern Patient* an interdisciplinary book bridging holistic and allopathic medicine together in a way that empowers patient/ doctor relationship.

These gems that I am so passionate about teaching have been infused in a book that I can refer to my clients as a reference of yoga and self-care practices and empowerment. Dreams are fulfilled, lives are impacted, big stuff happen. All because someone took the chance to just go for it.

Due to being a military spouse and the possibility of consistently relocating along with being a mother, I've had to adjust my career to be location independent and in a way that it can thrive from anywhere. I now write programs and lead yoga teacher trainings across the nation in therapeutic and adaptive flow yoga. I facilitate much of my work virtually and offer services online, in client's homes, and at local studios.

 I take every opportunity to meet and connect with others to discover ways that we can collaborate and empower our community. Furthermore, I have learned lessons in slowing down, in staying motivated, that written contracts are a big deal and matter, in trusting myself, and that whenever there is resistance it is affirmation that I am exactly where I need to be.

MelMarie LLC was built on the devotion to others, the courage to show up, and power yielded from self-care. My company has only thrived because of the Lord and who He has put into my life; those who have challenged me, those who have hurt me, those who presented me with self-doubt, those who celebrate me, those who encourage me, those who have invested in me.

It is through my humble gratitude that I do not work a job, but a ministry in educating the communities I come in contact with that they are their own best health advocate and to inspire them in living abundantly in all aspects of their being.

My journey has taught me to be flexible with my business and not to become too attached to any expectations. Expectation limits growth. I have goals and creative endeavours that I take my business on but I keep my mind open about what will blossom. Especially as I continue to make new connections and collaborative projects- I can only really project out within the next year. And I have found that even then it doesn't necessarily follow through.

I am the type of person who gets restless so I am never necessarily content in my goal accomplishment since I usually have an additional project or plan that I am working on executing. I like to stay motivated and see movement.

Melissa Aguirre

About The Author

Melissa Aguirre is a Nationally Registered Yoga Therapist, Certified Energy Medicine and MBSR Practitioner specializing in scientifically based Holistic health practices and education. Her passion for serving those who serve has led to the creation of her mindfulness based yoga therapy programs that serve the military population along with multiple wellness workshops and classes in Holistic healing to her national audience.

Melissa is a wellness speaker and contributing author for yoga therapy case studies continuing to impact optimal patient care and sustainable lifestyle choice. Her influence and support to charity events and Holistic health summits define her as a true asset and advocate to sustainable wellness.

In her free time, Melissa loves the little things; cozy evenings, her cats, journaling, her faith, movement, chai, sweaters with thumbholes, her daughter's snuggles, spending time with husband who keeps her rooted and inspired.

www.melmarieyoga.com

Twitter: @melmarieyoga

The Why, The What & The How

Being selected to write this chapter is an honour. Now, what knowledge do I impart with you? I have been sitting here wondering just what would you want to learn? What stage of business are you at?

So, I put a call out on Facebook and asked the question:

"If you were reading a book written by successful business women, what would you want to read about?" "What information would you want them to share with you?"

And, the questions you want answered were:-

What books do you recommend people read?

My advice is to read everything, not just the books that I list here, read every book on every subject. I say this because every person has something to teach you. And, every person will teach you something different.

- *Start with Why* by Simon Sinek
- *Think and Grow Rich* by Napoleon Hill
- *Business at the Speed of Thought* by Bill Gates
- *Instant Cashflow* by Brad Sugars
- **The Lean Startup** by Eric Ries
- **The 4-Hour Workweek** by Timothy Ferriss
- **Rework** by Jason Fried
- **The E-Myth Revisited** by Michael E. Gerber
- **The Alchemist** by Paulo Coelho
- **The $100 Startup** by Chris Guillebeau
- **Delivering Happiness** by Tony Hseih
- *The Millionaire Fastlane* by MJ DeMarco
- **Purple Cow** by Seth Godin
- **Mastery** by Robert Greene
- **Influence: The Psychology of Persuasion** by Robert B Cialdini

- *Good to Great* by Jim Collins
- *Crush it!* by Gary Vaynerchuk
- *We Are Market Basket: The Story of the Unlikely Grassroots Movement That Saved a Beloved Business* by Daniel Korschun and Grant Welker
- *Everybody Matters: The Extraordinary Power of Caring for Your People Like Family* by Bob Chapman and Raj Sisodia
- *How to Fly A Horse: The Secret History of Creation, Invention, and Discovery* by Kevin Ashton
- *The Compass and The Nail: How the Patagonia Model of Loyalty Can Save Your Business, and Might Just Save the Planet* by Craig Wilson
- *The Revenue Growth Habit: The Simple Art of Growing Your Business by 15% in 15 Minutes Per Day* by Alex Goldfayn
- *Boss Life: Surviving My Own Small Business* by Paul Downs
- *Reclaiming Conversation: The Power of Talk in a Digital Age* by Sherry Turkle
- *America's Bank: The Epic Struggle to Create the Federal Reserve* by Roger Lowenstein
- *Misbehaving: The Making of Behavioral Economics* by Richard Thaler
- *How Music Got Free: What Happens When an Entire Generation Commits the Same Crime?* by Stephen Witt
- *Unfinished Business: Women Men Work Family* by Anne-Marie Slaughter
- *The Rise of the Robots: Technology and the Threat of Mass Unemployment* by Martin Ford
- *Losing the Signal: The Untold Story Behind the Extraordinary Rise and Spectacular Fall of Blackberry* by Jacquie McNish and Sean Silcoff
- *Digital Gold: The Untold Story of Bitcoin* by Nathaniel Popper
- *Presence: Bringing Your Boldest Self to Your Biggest Challenges* by Amy Cuddy

What are your tips for developing a successful business?

1. Work on yourself, personal development is KEY.

2. Work on your business and not in it.
3. Take a break. Rest. An overworked brain cannot function at full capacity.
4. PLAY! Play with life, play with family, play with your kids.
5. Employ people for their attitude and develop their skills – it is much easier to teach skills than attitude.
6. Build systems, systems and systems, then tweak and refine those systems.
7. Know your customers and know why they are buying from you.
8. Have several mentors, business mentors, marketing mentors, specialised mentors
9. Hire a business coach, a marketing coach, a specialised coach for what you need.
10. Understand your wealth profile, know exactly how you make money and then go do it.
11. Make sure you have a very clear vision
12. Understand the purpose of your business and the purpose of every decision you make

In your opinion, what are the most common mistakes new business owners make?

Not Understanding Business – Most people start out in business for a number of different reasons. Most of the time, they know everything about their trade, but nothing about running a successful business. Always have a plan. That plan needs to include business strategy, marketing, finances, and the team. Good plans will tell you who is doing what and when.

Forgetting To Work On Their Business – In order to grow a successful business, you will need to work on the business. If you are only working in the business, then all you have is a JOB. A job, that requires you to work longer hours than if you were employed by someone else. Working on the business includes designing and implementing systems, business strategies for growth and expansion, new customer markets, joint ventures, customer feedback and more. When your business is profitable enough, stop doing the technical work, step out and focus on building the business.

Needing To Control – If this is a hard one for you, because you like to have control, then I suggest you start to design and implement systems. This is where systems are marvellous. The people follow the system. This gives you the control that you need while the people follow all the steps to achieve the desired end result and ultimately Happy Customers.

If you don't let go, you'll struggle in your business and continually go through an expansion and retraction process until your business dies or you give up in frustration.

Always Blame The System, Never The Person – if something goes wrong in your business, always blame the system, never the person. The person is only following all the steps and the instructions that have been set out in the procedures manual.

Tip: the best people to create the systems are those who are doing the actual work. If you open the business every morning, then you should be the one who explains how to do it.

Have you ever wanted to give up? What got you through?

I have never wanted to give up. I have been very overwhelmed at times and needed to take a rest. Go and do other things, like watch a movie, listen to some music, hang out with friends, but I have always kept going. When things have not worked out, or ideas haven't worked, I would take a break, have a rest, call my mentor and have a chat with him and then come back to the drawing board and fresh eyes.

What makes people successful?

Every time, I am asked this question, my answer is always the same. Every successful person solves problems. I also tell people that I've learnt that success is multifaceted and that mastering one principal of success or one area of your life isn't going to take you to the top – you need to be constantly learning. The more you learn, the more you master, the more successful you become. But, if I did have to identify one of the most important success strategies, it would be this. Find successful people and do the same thing until you get the same results. To be successful you need to be passionate and consistently positive in everything you do – believe in your end goal and expect the very best from yourself, your staff and your clients.

When you are not working, what do you like to do in your free time?

I love dancing, watching the stars at night. Every day I love listening to Jazz and every afternoon I love watching the sun set. I will stop what I am doing and go outside just to see the sunset every day. I love listening to earth's music, the music that is given to us by the earth, such as the sounds of the birds, or the wind blowing through the trees, the oceans as they break on the shoreline. Some people will go to an art gallery just to see a landscape painting I love to look at earth's art. Look out into the distance and you will see beautiful landscapes, you will see families having fun together and connecting, beautiful birds, picturesque scenes. This is earth's art and I like to admire earth's art every day. Everyday there is something new to look at, and every day there is a gorgeous piece of art to be admired.

What are the qualities of Great Leaders?

Successful leaders are visionaries. They hold a very strong vision and lead and influence others. They are confident and believe in themselves and in their own ability. They set and achieve goals, make decisions, learn from mentors and coaches, engage people to complement their own strengths and weaknesses, and most importantly, they delegate. A Great Leader gets on well with others, are customer focused, they love solving problems and spend time working on developing and growing the business. Great leaders show tenacity, a willingness to learn, an acceptance of different people, they have great self-discipline, and the adaptability to change. Great Leaders have a great attitude.

Formal education or learn as you go, which is better?

Both! I have done both and recommend both. There are times that you need to go and get a formal education and there are times that you can just learn it as you go. With everything changing all the time, it is essential that you run a business in accordance with the law, banking requirements and to a standard that enables you to compete effectively. Many business people are in business because of their trade or expertise in one area or another. Just because you are good at your trade, does not make you good at running a successful business. Issues that arise, especially when you start to employ people, are complicated and require substantial knowledge. Such as, business planning, marketing, the law, industrial relations, accounting, communications and occupational health and safety are all areas that can be studied at the highest levels. I have been formally trained in many areas of business and I have applied all my teachings in every area of my business.

Now, when you have a vision and there are no formal trainings being offered, then you really do have to learn on the go. The best way to do that is to find a mentor, someone who has done what you want to do and get them to guide you. I have read books and applied the knowledge that I have learnt from reading. I have also applied the knowledge that I have learnt from my mentor just through discussions with him. Every course I did, I learnt something and applied what I had learnt to my business.

What is your background?

You can be assured of the quality of information as I have been formally trained in: Business Management, Event and Festival Management, Workplace Assessor and Trainer, Business Office skills and administration, NLP Master Practitioner, Change Therapist, Transforming Communication Instructor, Life Coaching, Justice of the Peace (Qualified) St John ambulance First Aid Certificate, and I have a Blue Card for QLD.

You can be assured of the accuracy of the skills and knowledge being shared here, as I have had over twenty years of real, hands on, raw experience out in the field in all areas of communication, business, and life coaching. Areas of relevant experience has been acquired through working in industries such as manufacturing, hospitality, retail, direct sales, natural therapy, training and development, seminar logistics, debt collection, telecommunications, event coordinator, customer service, finance, investing, administration, telephone counselling, and management.

How many books have you written chapters for?

I have been asked to contribute my story to 4 separate books and am now a

Best Selling Published Author. The book titles are:

- *Inspired to Success* by Sandy Forster
- *Dare to Live* by Diane Carter
- *I Choose to be Me, I Choose to be Free* by Di Coop
- *Great Women Rise* by Ania Notoa

I have been writing and contributing chapters to two book series:

- *Sources of Wisdom* Vol 1 – Vol 6 – Denise Baron
- *Nurtured Women Books* Series Vol 1 – Vol 6 – Kathie Holmes

I also wrote and published my own book

- *Communication Impact* by Stacey Huish

Have you ever been a speaker?

Yes! I have been a guest speaker at three significant events.

- Dream It Up Festival - This is where we inspire high schools kids to 'Dream It Up" and go for what they want to do in life. Dream Big and make it happen.
- Great Women Rise Event - Great women sharing knowledge and wisdom with other great women. An honor to be on the stage.
- Shine Entrepreneurs Event - Magnificent event sharing what it takes to be a successful entrepreneur.

What is your Vision for the World?

Ever since I was 5 years old, I have held a strong my vision of building homes and schools for children all over the world. I have known since a very young age that this was and still is today my life purpose. My life's journey has taken me on many different paths and I have always returned to my purpose of building homes and schools. I have taught numerous people from all walks of life and impacted lifelong change as a result. Working in so many different roles throughout my life I have settled into my life's passion and LOVE...... I AM committed to the commitment of those around me and to the success that shines as a result.

How important is it to listen to your customer and meet customer needs?

Very important! Let me tell you a story of a first-hand experience with this. What I wanted to do was to run communication skills training. I had gone and learnt these communication skills and wanted everybody in the world to learn them also. So, I put up flyers on notice boards, ads in newsletters and magazines. No one showed up. No one wanted communication skills, what they did want was Parenting Skills covering topics such as How do you get your child to listen to you?

So, I changed the name of the course, put up all the flyers again and the course was booked out. Do you know what I taught them? That is right! Communication skills, because how you get your child to listen to you is by listening to them. I taught them all the communication skills and their relationships with their kids and their spouse improved. Parenting is all about communication.

What is the most important thing you have learnt about succeeding in business?

Enjoy the journey!

What is the biggest mistake you have made in business? What did you learn?

The biggest mistake I ever made in business is that I tried to fit in with other groups of people. I would turn up to business networking events, I was never meant to fit in, I was meant to gather my own tribe of people who were aligned with the vision and lead them. I worked this out eventually.

What do you love most about being in business?

I love that business is a form of self-expression. Everything I do is an expression of the love that I have for all the people in the world.

What Key Questions should you ask before developing a marketing strategy?

The first question to always ask is "What problem are you solving?" Then go to the next set of questions which are: Who? Why? What? Where? When? How?

What is the current project you are working on?

Right now, as I write this chapter for you to read, I am working on a book project entitled: 1000 Ripple Effects. This book project is about bringing stories and much needed wisdom to the kids who have no one. You have heard the saying "It takes a village to raise a child" well, I am creating that village. I am gathering 1000 people to write and share their story in this book. The context/subject of the book is all about - Sharing a pearl of wisdom with a child who does not have a mum or a dad. "1000 Ripple Effects" is creating a ripple effect for the people reading it. The stories in this book will be read by many people. The stories are designed to uplift, restore faith in humanity, and touch the hearts of many. The money raised from this book will then be used to create ripple effects in for our many projects. Build Self sustainable communities, build certified organic farms, provide employment opportunities, finish building the hospital and provide parenting skills training.

Not only are we creating 1000 ripple effects for the kids, but we are also creating 1000 ripple effects for all the authors as well. Each author will be presented with abundant opportunities to be interviewed on radio and on TV about the work that they do and how their work benefits the people in the community. The longer term vision is that that kids who read these stories will eventually come back to me and say "hey, Stacey, I have this idea for a great business!" and I will say to them, that is fantastic and you need to go and speak with "_____" in our village. These kids will eventually learn from the people who write the chapters in the book.

Have you had any experience in putting books together before?

Yes! A few years ago now, I had a vision that I would write a book on the importance of communication. When I really sat with this project, I understood that the community needed to write this book, not me. The people reading this book would be able to relate to the people in the community, they will share something in common, as they were the ones who had all the stories about the importance of communication. There are only so many stories that I have, and I do not have all of them. So, I gathered over 30 authors who all wrote stories for this book. I then learnt (self-taught) how to put a collaboration book together and print it. This has been a very valuable learning process.

Communication Impact by Stacey Huish

What is Wealth Dynamics? And What is a Wealth Profile?

Wealth Dynamics and Wealth Profiling was first discovered and used by Rodger Hamilton. Wealth Dynamics is a wealth profiling system utilizing in a psychometric test to assess your personality, strengths, productivity, values and group behaviour, to determine your most natural way to build wealth and a team of people around you.

A Wealth Profile is a profiling system that matches your personality, natural style and talents with each of the eight ways of creating wealth and uncovering, which path to wealth is the right one for you.

I've tried options trading (because others had made money doing this) but it didn't work for me. I went to all the business seminars, make money with real estate seminars, but what they were doing was teaching their wealth strategy and how they made money, which will work for some, but not for everyone. Certainly, not for me.

Once I did my wealth profile, once I understood how I made money, then set about doing it, I had success!

What does a wealth profile test give you?

After approximately 15 minutes you will have been given a report that is sent to your email inbox that tells you:

1. Your wealth profile
2. Successful people who share the same wealth profile as you
3. The top entrepreneurs you are most like.
4. Your strengths and weaknesses as a wealth creator
5. How to build your wealth foundation
6. Your moment of wealth creation
7. How to create value using your profile
8. The values you need to own
9. How you need to leverage yourself to create your wealth
10. How you secure your cash flow
11. The 6 steps you need to take to build your wealth

The Benefits of Wealth Dynamics

When you understand wealth dynamics and wealth profiling, you'll discover a way for you to build your wealth and a team around you, which comes naturally to you, so it's fun and sustainable. You'll be following a proven path, which others similar to you have already followed, and achieved success with.

You'll understand where to invest your time, and how to identify the right role models. You'll also begin to attract the opportunities and people who will help you build your wealth. To truly understand the benefits of wealth dynamics and wealth profiling, it's also important to understand wealth.

What Are The Eight Wealth Profiles?

There are eight different wealth profiles you can choose to build your wealth with. When you know your wealth profile, you'll know which game to choose and play. These are the 8 wealth profiles and the global entrepreneurs who follow the profiles strategy.

Creator... Bill Gates, Larry Ellison, Richard Branson
Star... Martha Stewart, Anthony Robbins, Oprah Winfrey
Supporter... Rudolph Giuliani and Jack Welch
Dealmaker... Donald Trump, Rupert Murdoch
Trader... George Soros
Accumulator... Warren Buffet
Lord... J D Rockefeller, J Paul Getty
Mechanic... Ray Kroc, Sam Walton

To find out more about the 8 different profiles and which profile you fit into get started now by following this link: **http://tinyurl.com/jy7rq2p.** This link will take you to a profiling test that has a combination of multiple choice and short answer questions. Here you will be able to discover your wealth profile and the 6 steps you need to take to build your wealth. All, from the comfort of your own home or office.

Stacey Huish

About The Author

Stacey Huish is a strong powerful game changer, a speaker, educator, author and lover of life.

I'm a free spirit, who is affectionately known as the "Game Changer". I am an earth healer, a heart healer, raising the vibration of love to help as many people as possible to live passionate and purpose filled lives, awaken the planet and enable the divine purpose of the universe to unfold.

That is My Life!
That is my purpose for me being here!

I am a Social Entrepreneur, 1 Million Women Ambassador and a Change Maker. A woman who puts her heart and soul into everything she does. I'm a woman who loves people and loves life.

www.1000rippleeffects.com

Success: Profit Or Purpose And Personal Fulfilment?

Introduction

Thesaurus: Synonym of Success - Prosperity

"Prosperity doesn't mean that you will have wealth, health and happiness. The best way to explain prosperity is to say it is like when a rosebud flowers and opens up, and it shares its fragrance. That's the moment, which lasts a few days, when a rose flower is prosperous. When a man or woman is prosperous, it is the fragrance of security, grace, depth, character, and truthfulness that a person can share. Like a candle emits light, a human emits prosperity."

A quote from Yogi Bhajan, the Founder of Kundalini Yoga 12/26/97 from

"Success and the Spirit: An Aquarian Path to Prosperity"

What is success?

From a young age we are programmed to think of success in monetary terms, in terms of wealth and financial prosperity. We are accustomed to think that a CEO of a Corporation or a Self-Made Millionaire has achieved more success than we have because they have gained position, influence and affluence.

At school we strive for the best exam results; not only in Australia but all around the world, students sit for their final high school certificate (High School Certificate or equivalent) at aged 17/18; the results that arrive in an envelope at the end of their education is considered the reflection of their entire school career and define how successful they have been.

After school many of us will aim for the best university to study for the best course that will get us the best career. We'll want the best job that will lead us to the best promotion and the highest salary. We'll want the best partner, the best house in the best street. We'll then repeat the cycle through our kids hoping they'll achieve more than we did. This is how we measure our success.

There is nothing wrong with any of this provided we don't lose sight of the end goal. That end goal has to be personal fulfilment and a life of contentment. That is true success. Easier said than done one might assume, but if we go within ourselves to discover our life's purpose then the end goal will be within our grasp.

It would be fascinating to survey CEOs of top corporations as to whether they feel have reached a level of success or whether they are continually striving to reach that level. In their search for success are they in fact working such long hours at the detriment of everything else in their life that real success will never be theirs?

It is time we measured success in different terms – in terms of fulfilment through your work and in terms of finding joy in what you do. Let's talk about a successful business owner as one whose mission is to make a positive change in the world, be it within their community or even on a global level.

We generally believe a company to be successful if it has achieved profitability and growth. But how often does a corporation achieve that success, without consciously considering its company ethos and culture amongst its staff? How often do corporations take from staff, suppliers and even their customers in search of that bottom line profit margin but give very little back? A truly successful company is one that recognizes the value of partnerships with its suppliers, staff and customer base, not one that exists solely for soaring profit margins. In the world of retail, there is a growing movement away from fast fashion and an industry that has profited from the spoils of factory slave labour to achieve its success. Conscious Consumerism is a flourishing trend that is prompting major retailers to develop ethical practices and to invest in sustainable production methods.

This has been the background to the creation of Temples and Markets, an online store I founded in early 2015. I wanted to create a business that provided an enjoyable buying experience at every point for the customer; one that provides the customer with the added halo effect that when they shop they are doing some good in the global community. It is in essence what I call the Win-Win effect.

The measure of success for my business is two-fold. It provides a win-win for the customer but for the suppliers too. The core value is that the suppliers – Artisan Groups, Emerging Designers and Social Enterprise whose creations I showcase in store – share in its achievements. Their stories are told on the website bringing them closer to the consumer in a way that is rare in the often cold world of E-commerce.

My Story

So many of us, meander through life from one job to another or from one business to another striving to find our life's purpose. It may have been staring us in the face for a long time but fear or self-doubt prevented us from grabbing it. And so it was with me.

From a very young age I knew, as corny as it sounds, that I wanted to make a difference. Having studied history at university and being a staunch humanitarian, I am often affected emotionally by the world's injustices. During university I dreamed of doing something worthwhile with my life, but as a graduate in London in the late 80s I just had to find a job. I found myself in the cutthroat world of chain store buying and merchandising, not many opportunities to make a difference in the world there. Although I worked up the ladder, I was pleased to turn my back on that life when I left the U.K in 1997 to travel the world.

I spent 5 months trekking the well-worn backpacking path of some of S.E

Asia's most visited countries. It was during that trip that I expanded my knowledge of how hard the world is and in contrast, how charmed my life is. The region found its way into my heart and has never left. Since that first trip I have returned to Thailand, Indonesia, Malaysia, China, Hong Kong and Singapore, Vietnam and Laos many times.

It would be reasonable to say I'm addicted to travelling, shopping and eating my way through South East Asia and get back there as often as I can. The region is so full of contrasts – from the buzz of the night markets to the serenity of a resort spa, from a visit to an ancient Buddhist temple followed by a ride in a Tuk-Tuk through noisy bustling streets. I love the smells of Lemongrass and Frangipani and the tastes of hot curries and tropical fruit. I love eating noodle soup for breakfast and satay sticks by a pool.

Most of all, lingering memories from travelling in S.E Asia have come from the gracious and warm people I've met along the way. I have never failed to be awestruck by the resilience, strength and astounding creativity of the people I spent time getting to know. In countries such as Vietnam and Cambodia, where recent history has caused great hardships, horror seems to have begat beauty. Much has happened in those 20 years since I first backpacked through South East Asia. During that trip it became clear that on returning to the rat race life in London was never going to be an option and I migrated to Sydney, Australia.

Frequent travel, motherhood and a brush with the real possibility of an early demise in the form of breast cancer at the age of 36 have shaped who I am today. Cancer was simultaneously the best and worst thing to have happened to me. Ten years on I live with the real possibility of a recurrence but with life so short I am more conscious of a desire for fulfilment, positivity and contentment.

I tried the corporate world for a few years in advertising but I don't have the make up to work for somebody else. I have a fierce independent entrepreneurial streak and a creative personality. Furthermore, to avoid a cancer recurrence, I was determined to avoid stress where possible and instead follow a regime of daily exercise and an organic diet. After my recovery I looked for a creative outlet whereby I could fulfil my own destiny.

I'd always had an interest in interior design and formed an Interior Design and Project Management company. Doesn't that sound like a glamorous and creative existence? Or perhaps you're reading this and have experience of the building industry and you're probably laughing at the idea, that I thought I'd avoid stress in that world. And you'd be right to be laughing. I'm laughing now at the thought of it. I literally believed I could make a difference in this male dominated arena; even act as a client advocate when it came to negotiating on their behalf with tradespeople. In reality the only positivity I got out of that life was at the end of a project; it was always a delight to see a transformation of a property that I'd played a part in creating. But the path to getting there was never without its battles and upsets.

Suffice to say it took a long time to realize that the path to success lay in recognising and following my passion. Everything that came prior, be it illness or failure in business, was part of the journey to get me to that point. If I was to achieve success in terms of fulfilment, the timing had to be right. In early 2015 the catalyst presented itself and the concept of Temples and Markets, an idea that had been milling around in my mind for a long while, came to fruition.

Temples and Markets

During a trip to Siem Reap in Cambodia in January 2015, I stumbled upon a small boutique selling handmade jewellery. Had I not been dining at a café in the same laneway as the boutique, chances are I would never have come across it. The window display was striking – bold and contemporary jewellery pieces fashioned from local seeds such as I'd never seen before. I was drawn in and learnt the story behind the jewellery and the designer, Rany, who created the pieces. She became the impetus for Temples and Markets.

Rany returned to Siem Reap after a failed marriage in India. She'd been away for 4 years. Sadly her parents didn't approve of divorce and she wasn't welcomed back into the family home.

Times were tough and Rany struggled to find work. She'd always been creative but as the oldest of 7 kids had never had the opportunity to go to design or art school. She saw potential in the small, colourful seeds on the road in Siem Reap and collected some, determined to turn them into something beautiful. It took time to work out how to make holes in the seeds; she borrowed a drill and cut her hands. She persevered though and made her first pair of earrings followed by a small collection that she shared with her friends. They were impressed and urged her to make more.

Fast-forward to today and she now has 7 local women handcrafting the beautiful jewellery she designs in the small workshop behind her boutique. I've watched them, sitting cross-legged on the floor, drilling into every tiny seed with meticulous care.

Selecting the seeds is a painstaking process - each has to be the perfect size, shape and symmetry to fit with her designs. Rany used to collect them herself; now the local villagers collect them for her.

I'd heard so many stories in S.E Asia like Rany's, of survival spawning creativity and success. The time was right to bring these stories to an audience outside the region. By telling their stories via an online store that showcases their creations, I have developed a platform that literally helps trade artisans and emerging designers, often marginalised or from poverty stricken communities, into a better life.

I already knew there was a market for unique finds from my travels. After previous trips to Thailand or Vietnam I'd come back wearing a piece of jewellery or a bag and repeatedly be asked, "Where did you get that?" I'd watch the enquirer's face drop when I told them "that comes from Thailand

and isn't available in Australia". An idea formulated in my mind that I should give my fabulous finds access to a market outside of S.E Asia and expose the emerging designers and artisan groups I met to a wider audience outside of the region.

I should add that when I'd returned from travelling I'd often reminisce about the myriad of creations I'd seen and regretted not buying for reasons of budget or luggage space. I was aware that this affliction was exclusively mine and that there'd be a market of other travellers who'd also returned home from S.E Asia with what I call "Buyers Regret." In November 2015 the online store Temples and Markets went live. It was a year in the making – sourcing products, designing the website, product photography and copy writing, which saw me working into the early hours for weeks on end in the run up to launch. But I wouldn't have had it any other way. This was my baby and I felt immense pride in how it turned out and the positive feedback it received.

Visitors to the site early on were surprised at the wide range of exquisite and unique products available. Perhaps they were expecting cheapie souvenir type merchandise that we all know is found all over Thai or Vietnamese markets. On the contrary, Temples and Markets show cases pieces across its collections that have a clear designer element to them. Within a few short months Temples and Markets evolved, initially the concept had been to expose emerging designers and artisans with that oriental twist to a larger audience outside of the region.

Quickly it became increasingly about affecting positive change in the region that I love. I added Social Enterprises such as the *Senhoa Foundation* whose tagline is "Employ, Empower, Emancipate" Proceeds from the sales of exquisite Senhoa Jewellery go directly to the rehabilitation and education of young women who are vulnerable to or are survivors of slavery in Cambodia.

I added *Smateria*, founded by two Italian designers who had two very clear objectives: to create a beautiful, high-quality product using 'bizarre' materials, and to employ Cambodian workers in a fair and sustainable way, giving priority to women and mothers. Their stylist bags are fashioned from recycled fishing nets or leather sofa offcuts.

Zsiska Jewellery was always going to be featured in the store; their colourful vibrant necklaces I'd been wearing for years had been the subject of many a "Where did you get that" enquiries. Dutch designer Siska founded her namesake company in 1992 in Cha-Am near Bangkok. The fourteen women with whom Siska started the company still work for Zsiska today. It is a family affair with most of their family members and children joining the company to work in a social environment.

It didn't take long for other Social Organisations, who fit within the premise of Temples and Markets, to approach me for inclusion. I've been only too delighted to support them and so proud that they'd heard about my work and its purpose. Orphaned during the horror days of Cambodia's Khmer Rouge, Chanta Theon heads up *Angkor Bullet Jewellery*, a group of home-based artisans, some vulnerable and disabled, who reside in a small community around 30 minutes from Phnom Penh. Decided they would transform bullet casings, a symbol of war, into unique designer jewellery. From horror comes beauty.

Despite significant advances in its economy and a burgeoning tourism industry 20% of Cambodians still live under the poverty line. Furthermore Cambodia has a reputation as one of the worst places in the world for child prostitution and human trafficking. The minimum monthly wage in Cambodia as well as Vietnam and Laos is currently under $150. By partnering with more social enterprises, which are empowering the locals in these countries through training and fair work opportunities, I am contributing to creating a sustainable future for them and their families.

Knowing that I can make a tangible difference to the lives of these trained artisans, by showcasing their creations, gives me that sense of fulfilment and satisfaction that I've been searching for since those university days. Their stories are now closely inter-weaved with my story. To be in a position whereby I can literally help them, their families and their wider communities out of poverty through my online store has brought me to a point in my life where I feel extremely fortunate to have found my life's purpose. This is success as I see it; this is the end goal, the sense of prosperity and personal growth, attained by doing well and giving back.

Temples and Markets presents a win-win for everybody involved – the artisans of course, the customers and for myself. It's simply a joyous feeling knowing you're contributing positively to the global community.

Life feels better for me when I help

Through a Women in Business networking group I have connected with several female entrepreneurs in recent times, who like myself have been fortunate to have found their life's purpose through their socially conscious businesses. Roz Campbell's story resonated with me greatly as her company Tsuno also helps disadvantaged women in developing countries.

How many of us have ever given a second thought to what women and girls do when they can't afford or don't have access to sanitary products? Roz had been researching the feminine hygiene market and heard about an Australian based charity providing education scholarships to girls in Sierra Leone, one of the world's poorest countries, called One Girl. After sending their first bunch of girls to school, they soon realised girls were missing up to a week of school every month because of their periods. They would fall behind at school, struggle in exams and eventually drop out.

Roz had heard heartbreaking stories of women resorting to rags, newspaper, kitchen sponges, leaves and sadly even tree bark as a feminine hygiene solution. Roz felt compelled to help because, in her own words,

"Life feels better for me when I help, and this is how I've decided to do so".

Roz sourced a sanitary product from a manufacturer working with sustainable fibres. They make bamboo and corn fibre disposable sanitary pads. The structure of the fibre is quite hollow, so it has lots of room for absorbing moisture, which is perfect for pads, drawing the moisture away from your body. In 2014 she ran a crowd funding campaign that saw 1400 women pre-ordering her sustainable and eco-friendly pads, giving her enough money for the first shipment. But Tsuno is much more than a company that sells fully sustainable disposable sanitary pads. Roz donates 50% of net profits from the sale of the Tsuno pads to charities helping to empower women in the developing world. She has an agreement with the One Girl charity that believes every girl on the planet has a right to education.

Roz's statement "Life feels better for me when I help" is such a simple phrase but it encompasses how I feel about success. By helping others we are helping ourselves.

Sally Maree Hetherington is a good friend of mine; we've become close through our aligned values. I connected with her after learning about her work for the Not for Profit organization Human and Hope Association based in Siem Reap, Cambodia. HHA empowers locals through training; education and community support so that they may create sustainable futures for themselves and break the cycle of poverty. Sally and I have partnered together to bring some of the handicrafts made by the Association's sewing graduates to my store.

Sally is a shining example of an inspiring successful woman in business. As she says, her success lies in the fact that she worked hard to actively put herself out of a job! From 2012 – 2016 Sally worked tirelessly as Operations Manager at Human and Hope Association, now entirely run by Cambodians. She always intended to step aside when the time was right leaving the locals to continue what she helped to build.

With the support of local staff Sally helped to build up the grassroots organization so that it was a professional, trustworthy and effective Non-Government Organisation for the community to reach out to donors for support. They registered Human and Hope Association as an official NGO, created a Khmer team of paid employees, developed a donor database, initiated various programs with the aim to alleviate social issues, initiated weekly training sessions, developed a sewing business and other sources of income and built a permanent location for HHA. Sally joined Human and Hope Association with the aim of helping the organization and staff reach their full potential, and then step back. She is incredibly proud of the achievements of her team and the fact that they have worked so hard that she could become redundant. She cried many tears the day she left, although she is still involved at board level for fundraising. But she insists selflessly it was never about her. It has always been about empowering the team with knowledge, skills and confidence so that she is no longer needed. If that's not the definition of success I don't know what is.

Life has, for me, gone full circle. I began my working life in department store retail buying and merchandising in the U.K. Fast forward 20 years later and I am living in Sydney but back in retail buying, this time sourcing for my own online store. But there's a stark contrast between then and now as today I am part of the growing movement of ethical retailers, and part of something good.

The world is changing and consumers are becoming increasingly more conscious about their purchasing decisions, wanting to know where their purchases come from and who made them. Many larger fashion retailers are already recognizing this and endeavouring to treat their production workers ethically. Eventually the tide will flow against any who are still exploiting their workers.

It is clear that businesses with a purpose are the ones that achieve true success, not just success derived from an increasing profit margin. Whilst it is crucial to work towards a healthy profit margin if a business is to make a change in the world for good, that company must have a healthy perspective on what will benefit its customer, its suppliers and the community at large.

To have found my purpose at this stage in my life feels remarkable. The need to make a difference in the world had been staring me in the face from an early age and I've finally grabbed it. My personal success comes from the fulfilment I'm enjoying for the first time in my working life. There's immense satisfaction knowing I've made a woman feel good about herself when she wears a beautiful piece of unique jewellery I've sourced. In turn that same woman can enjoy the satisfaction of knowing she has contributed to the increased prosperity of the talented woman who made it. In essence I am creating an ever-increasing circle of women who are affecting each other's lives in a positive way through trade. The more people whose lives I improve the more successful I will become. As long I am contributing to the increasing prosperity of the creative, strong and resilient artisans in the countries I love, the more fulfilled I will be.

"Success Isn't About How Much Money You Make. It's about the Difference you Make in People's Lives" a quote from Michelle Obama, USA First Lady 4/9/2012 DNC Convention.

Judith Treanor

About The Author

Judith Treanor originates from a town close to London, England. Judith graduated in History at university before spending several years working in the Buying and Merchandising departments of House of Fraser, Harrods and Debenhams. Essentially she has been sourcing suppliers and product for over 25 years.

In 1997 Judith left England as a slightly older than average backpacker to explore the world before migrating to Sydney, Australia. It was during those travels that the region of South East Asia found its special place in her heart and has never left.

Fast forward to the present and Judith is a proud mum to one amazing 12 year old son, who never fails to make her proud, and one floppy eared slightly crazy cocker spaniel cross. Judith practices Kundalini Yoga and is a serious foodie. She frequently gets itchy feet and travels overseas as often as she can. If she's near a beach Judith loves nothing more than taking a beach walk in the quiet of an early morning so she can make friends with the local dogs.

Travel, motherhood and serious illness have shaped who Judith is today. In 2006, aged 36 she was diagnosed with Breast Cancer, simultaneously the best and worst thing to have happened to her. Aware how short life is Judith is determined to live hers feeling healthy, contented and fulfilled. She has a fierce creative streak and an entrepreneurial nature.

She feels fortunate to have recently found her life's purpose - making a difference in the lives of others in the countries of S.E Asia that she fell in love with almost 20 years ago. She is now part of the growing ethical shopping movement. Judith's love of S.E Asia is showcased through her online store Temples and Markets which launched last November 2015.

You can contact Judith via:

Email: contactus@templesandmarkets.com.au

Website: www.templesandmarkets.com

Social Media:

https://www.facebook.com/templesandmarkets

https://www.instagram.com/templesandmarkets

https://au.pinterest.com/templesmarkets/

Roz at Tsuno:

http://www.tsuno.com.au/

Sally at the Human and Hope Association:

http://www.sallyhetherington.com/

http://www.humanandhopeassociation.org/

Starting A Business With No Money

When I ask, "why don't you start a business?" do you think to yourself, you need money to start a business and I don't have any? Most people do. There is a common misconception that you must have money to open a business and for lots of businesses you would be correct. You can't open a shop on the street corner without cash for deposits, bonds, fit outs, etc. But does that apply in all circumstances? No. Can you really start a business with very little or no money? Yes absolutely. Does it involve some creative problem and thinking outside the box? Yes. Are you capable of that? Absolutely!

My story

I started my business with very, very little money to put down. Yes, there might have been a few rules I skirted around in order to get started, and I am not condoning rule and law breaking, but I have the philosophy of "Ready, Fire, Aim" approach to entrepreneurship rather than "Ready, Aim, Fire." I have always been the kind of person that gets very excited by new business ideas and becomes a bit like a bull at a gate. I just can't wait to get started on making money. I love seeing an idea come to reality and people actually start buying it. So exciting! Consequently I am a little bit lenient on details.

Some people have an approach to business that needs to lay out all the finer details before commencing on a project. Whilst I really admire those people and those skills are very necessary in certain fields, like engineering. I would like to think engineers plan minute details when they are building a bridge, things could really come undone for them if they just started and thought, "we will figure it out as we go." We are lucky as entrepreneurs that we are allowed to be a little bit more flexible in our approach. So, we can have a brief plan and just get started, then we can adapt based on our customer's feedback and needs.

Here is what I did: I used to make a lot of fresh juices at home. I loved doing my own juice cleanses at home. The fresh fruits and vegetables always made me feel amazing, snapping me out of bad eating habits, helping to remove bloating and made my skin glow. The benefits were always incredible, but the juicing and cleaning was always a hassle. I thought to myself, there has to be other people out there that would love the benefits of a juice cleanse without the hassle of making them.

So I decided to get started. First of all I had to design recipes and menus. Then I had to sort out packaging and design a "program" so there was a process for people to follow. I had to meet with naturopaths and nutritionists to help me design recipes and program types. I had to get samples of packaging that I could use. What did all this cost me? Time, but not money.

I used my home juicer and did the first juicing for a few weeks from my home very early in the morning, then did the deliveries before my day job. Then I would go into my recruitment job, and come home at night, answer any customer emails, etc. Then start again early the next morning. It was tiring, but I was so high on the adrenaline of actually making my own money in my own business that it didn't matter. I knew it wasn't going to be this way forever and growth was the first priority on my mind. It wasn't replacing my salary as I didn't pay myself a wage in the business until about 3 years in. But I wanted to grow and do it as organically as possible.

Just like that, I was in business! The free media trials have led to orders on my website and I had money in my PayPal account that I could use to buy packaging, and get proper labels printed and grow my business. It was such a fantastic feeling that I'd managed to start something that people were paying for, and it was such a rush to actually be in business!

How you can do it too?

Start by finding your "genius". We all have value we can add to the world. Truly successful businesses are ones that genuinely add value to people's lives. Choose to approach your business as a method to share your genius with the world and add value to others, rather than looking at your business as a "get rich quick" scheme.

Questions to ask yourself?

What can I do really well? What can I do that would help other people enrich their lives? How can I do that with scale (help as many people as possible)? You don't have to only think in an altruistic sense, the value you could add could be done in a multitude of ways. Here are some examples to give you some perspective:

- A real estate investor provides affordable housing for people that can't afford to buy a property
- A hairdresser helps people look their best
- A learn to surf business helps people to find joy in doing something fun and exciting
- A nutrition consultant helps people feel their most energetic and vibrant
- An online fashion boutique owner helps people get the latest looks while shopping from the comfort of their home

Think about how you can add value to other people lives and where you can give your genius to the world.

The key is to believe in what you do...

Some people get freaked out by the idea of "selling". They will say to themselves, "oh, I could never do sales, I am not a salesperson." But the truth is we sell every day. The key is finding something you believe in so much that it doesn't even feel like selling. I recently met a lady who was so passionate for the product she sold that she just couldn't help herself trying to help people. She was a friend of a friend and we were away for the weekend.

Every single person we came across was an opportunity for her to help someone change their life. I was so impressed with her enthusiasm and thought if she talked to everyone she met in a day like that, when she bought petrol, groceries, went for a walk, picked the kids up from day care, and did this every day for 6 months, she would have touched so many potential customers for free. Her customers would then tell her friends and suddenly she has a market for her business with no advertising costs. The key is finding something that you really believe in. If you really believe you can truly add value to someone's life, and then you would not be "selling", you would be opening doors for people to change their lives.

When I was working full time, all I could think about was how insanely cool it would be and what an incredible rush it would be to have people actually spend their money on a product that I had created. I was working in a corporate job, wearing high heels and suits every day. I used to see myself in my comfy gym clothes as my job. I didn't want to be a personal trainer, but thought it would be so amazing if I had a job where I could wear what I wanted and be totally comfortable every day. This was a dream of mine, every day. Looking back I only really now realise the importance and gravity of my day dreaming. It was the consistent visualising and excitement that went with the imaginary pictures in my mind that manifested exactly what I dreamt about.

If business is what you want, then it is vital that you start living your life like it now. The importance of believing that you are already doing what you want, now. I don't mean going out and spending all your money in the belief that you already have loads of it. But, looking for opportunities, seeing things that you like other businesses doing and telling yourself that you will implement that in your business. Looking for marketing opportunities, looking at where your customers might congregate. You don't have to have an existing enterprise to do these things, you just need an idea and you can start acting as if you have the business already.

There is a book called, *The Magic of Believing*, by Claude M. Bristol. The ideas he presents are not new, it is in fact quite an old book, but I love the way he presents his perspective on how things have happened for him based on setting his new beliefs about his life, career, etc.

So visualise your new life running a successful business, what kind of person would you be? How would you hold yourself? How would you explain your business when you meet new people? How would you dress? What kind of books would you read? What kind of websites/networking groups would you be part of? How would your new life make you feel? Creating a new reality for yourself is a crucial step to becoming the business owner you want to be.

Marketing your business

The basis of any successful business is marketing. A lot of people will argue the basis is sales, or customers, but you won't have any of those if your customers don't know about you. The only way they will know about you is marketing. Now the idea of a marketing plan probably freaks a lot of people out, and rightly so. When I was doing my MBA and had to prepare marketing plans, they were a lot of work, a very detailed, very densely worded, a thickly bound document that looked great on a shelf but was never looked at again. You will need to have a very basic and simple understanding of marketing for your business. But it can be very simple, so don't panic. Here are the most important questions to address:

What makes me different?

This is called defining your Unique Selling Proposition (USP). It is why you are special compared to other peoples, what makes your product better than others, why should people spend their hard earned money on your product as opposed to someone else's. For my business, in the early stages I was the only juice cleanse company. So while it may seem that my USP was easy, it wasn't. A lot of people thought it was kind of crazy spending $300 on 5 day's worth of juice.

But my USP was focused on providing a very easy and very healthy way for people to cleanse their body, feel amazing and kick-start to a healthier lifestyle. Don't be afraid that your USP will change as your business evolves. A natural part of the business life cycle is competition, so as your business grows so will your competition. That may be direct replicas of your product or it may be competition for the consumer spend, for example as my business grew, direct competitors popped up with the same ideas offering the same products as my company did. As well as other options for people to do a detox program with things like herbs, AND options for people to do their own juicing at home. So I had to start providing something unique for my customers that was different to my direct and indirect competition. Now that business has changed our USP focuses on providing the freshest juice as we are still the only business offering daily delivery within 20km of CBD in Sydney, Melbourne and Brisbane.

Who are my customers?

You need to understand exactly the type of person that will buy from you. Are they just like you? Or completely different from you? What are their main motivations to buy? Is it because they want the latest fashions or perhaps they are a practical dresser that prefers to spend their money on computer games. Are they male or female? What kind of job do they have? What would they do on a Saturday night? Would they be out at the trendiest night spots or at home in bed after an exhausting day with the kids? Put yourself in your customer's shoes and really understand who they are. This is a really key step on your marketing plan. Once you have understood your customer you can better know where they will be and what they will do. So not only can you tailor your product/offering accordingly, you can spend your marketing dollars more efficiently and effectively as opposed to spending a lot of money in a blanket approach.

What do I need to say to those customers to help win business or maintain business?

Ok, now you have figured WHO your customers are, you understand how they tick, what they like and dislike, you can now figure out the message that you want to send to them. Don't be afraid to have different messages for different customers. For some people you might want to say something particular, and for another group of people it might be a different message.

How am I going to get in contact with those customers?

This is all about the how you are going to get your message across to your customers. So, it could be via social media, or TV advertising (if you have the budget!), maybe leaflet drops if you are a pizza place in a particular suburb, it could be calling childcare centres to get your sample products in the hands of time poor mums if you have a product that might help them. Be prepared to think laterally when you don't have a big budget. Once you completed the step of identifying your customer there might be something that your customer does that you can piggy back off, like do they do Yoga each week, so call the yoga studios and do a deal with them.

Building credibility

It's important to build credibility in your area of expertise, whether it is selling beauty products online or if you are a consultant for helping women achieve financial freedom. The easiest and cheapest way I have found to do this is blogging. Remember you don't have to position yourself as an "expert" on a particular topic, so don't stress that you don't have a degree or any qualifications, but you can definitely join the conversation. Use your blog to discuss current happenings in your arena, new research, what you do (e.g. your daily skincare routine, or your home recipes), your own experience with experts, etc. I don't have qualifications in nutrition or naturopathic remedies, although I consulted with them and used them heavily I was very self-educated on the topics. I read, read and re-read all the latest and greatest books on topics of natural health. So although I wasn't an "expert" I still felt that I was able to join the conversation and discuss theories, add in my opinion and my own experience.

Blogging only takes your time and your thinking. You can easily and quickly add additional credibility to your website or profile or store via blogging. You can add to your search rankings too with more material on your topic, so the search engines will love you.

My tips for starting a business as cost effectively as possible

Define your marketing plan as above – it may take some time to think about, but it will be the best and most profitable exercise you can do.

Starting the website – look at the free builder options available. Just search "free website builder" in your search engine and you will find there are quite a few basic options out there to get started. These days they are very easy to find your way through and to start developing. Remember you don't have to start with all the bells and whistles, just get started you can always upgrade later when you have some money in the bank.

Using PayPal – setting up a payment gateway can be expensive and fiddly, but the easiest and quickest way to start accepting money on your site is PayPal. It is a recognised brand and people feel comfortable with it, the merchant fees aren't the best, but once again, it is a great option to just get cracking and then you can spend some time setting up a different merchant gateway when you are more established.

Free media coverage – it's as simple as making a call. This was definitely a clincher for me in the early days, getting my product in the hands of media influencers I did by contacting PR agencies and media, it's just call away. I called all the magazines and asked for the beauty editor, I explained I had a juice cleanse that I really wanted them to try so it would be amazing if I could send them a free trial.

Be honest, act with integrity, share love and you will be rewarded. They are just people and they are always looking for new material to write about in magazines, so sell your products with your passion and they will be excited to write about it.

Asking suppliers questions – if you need samples, testers, etc.. don't be afraid to ask your potential suppliers for samples. They are in business too, so you as a potential new customer could be great news for them. They may not be willing, but you will be surprised at how many could be. You just need to ask.

Use Social Media – Using Twitter and Instagram are great ways to promote your product free of charge using hashtags. Set up your accounts for free and educate yourself a little on how the whole hashtag game works and you can start getting followers and people liking your posts. It all helps to spread the word.

Conclusion

Starting a business without much money is an achievable and rewarding path to success. Anyone that believes in themselves, and believes in their goals, like I did, can find their way into their own exciting venture. Find your own genius and create value for other people and you will find yourself skyrocketing to success.

Catherine Craig

About The Author

Catherine Craig is the owner of Schkinny Maninny. She has been in business almost a decade and started her company from scratch to million dollar plus revenues without any debt. She believes in healthy eating and clean lifestyle and how juicing can change your life.

If you would like some more info please just send me a message:

Email: catherine@schkinnymaninny.com.au

Create the Life You Want

Everyone has a story; everyone's story is interesting. Everyone's life has up and downs, successes and failures, they have felt both love and pain, and they have laughed and cried. I believe I can learn something from everyone's story.

At 49 my life story would take a little more than the chapter I have been allocated in this book, instead I want to share the journey I have been on over the last 4 years. Since 2012, I have been leading a very passionate and profitable life and I love it. That is not to say that I wasn't living a full life before that, but in 2012 something changed. Suddenly, I had put my foot on the accelerator and jumped onto a Formula One track. To understand the last 4 years, you first need to know a little of my history leading up to 2012.

I have always been a driven person, highly competitive and, some might say, a workaholic. I have also been willing to take risks, which is why I left a very rewarding career in marketing to start my journey into recruitment in 1999. At the time, I was the Marketing Manager in one of Australia's largest food marketers and manufacturers. As the Marketing Manager, I was responsible for a team of marketers and managing the recruitment process. The recruitment of staff became the bane of my existence!

What was so awful about it?

Firstly, whenever an employee left, it was always poorly timed. They always seemed to resign just when I needed something important done, and inevitably, the rest of the team had to work longer and harder to get it finished.

Secondly, the recruiters I was working with were consistently hard to deal with. They didn't understand me as a client; often, they didn't even bother to meet with me. I felt as though I was wasting time interviewing people who weren't even close to being right and I was getting frustrated. The candidates seemed to be treated like commodities, with the recruiters rarely considering the emotional toll involved with any career move, and that their poor service and mistreatment of candidates reflected poorly on my business.

Finally, these recruiters were too expensive for what they were delivering; A few CVs emailed to me, a few interviews arranged and then a big bill. Where was the expertise? Where was the service? Where was the care? Despite my growing distaste for dealing with recruiters, I had to admit that I needed them. I didn't have the time to sift through hundreds of resumes or the budget to run expensive advertising to find the right candidate.

The realisation of just how bad recruiters were dawned on me in one single, epiphanic moment. I was interviewing for a Brand Manager role within my marketing team. The recruiter, let's call him, "Mr Flick'n'Stick", had sent me the CV of a fantastic candidate. "Super Candidate" had years of great experience but he was a lot more senior than the role required. The recruiter told me, "Super Candidate" was willing to step into a more junior role because he had heard of me and my work, and wanted the opportunity to work with me.

I was pretty impressed with myself. This was my first big Marketing Manager role and hearing that someone had heard of me and was willing to take a step down in order to work in my team was a lovely stroke to my young ego. We've all been there, right? Freshly promoted, intending to build the perfect team and making a name for ourselves. Of course, I was happy to interview this well-credentialed and experienced candidate.

Within the first five minutes of the interview I was burning up with embarrassment. I had started the meeting feeling confident and after a few niceties, I said, 'Thanks for coming "Super Candidate". I hear that you're really interested in joining my team and working with me…' With a blank stare he replied, 'No, not really. I was told that there was a vacant Marketing Manager role. "Mr Flick'n'Stick" said that the business needs an experienced marketer because there is a capability issue.' My heart dropped. This guy was there for my job. He had been told by "Mr Flick'n'Stick" that the marketing team was underperforming. He had no idea who I was or what brands the company owned.

Excuse me while I pick up the pieces of my shattered ego...

We had both been set up. We call this the 'foil' in marketing. You set up a bad comparison to make your product, service or in this case, candidate, look good. By sending me candidates who didn't fit the brief, "Mr Flick'n'Stick" was making me desperate to fill the role and therefore, more likely to hire someone who was not right but was simply the 'best' of what I had to choose from. Mr Flick'n'Stick was showing "Super Candidate" that he should really consider some of the other roles presented to him, otherwise he may end up working in a lower level job for a new manager like me.

I couldn't believe this recruiter's lack of processes and ethics. There was no partnership or expertise sharing and I was angry at the time wasted and the disrespect shown to both the candidate and me. This experience had well and truly burst my bubble and planted the seeds for my first business.

About 18 months after this incident I resigned from my job. With no idea about running a small business, let alone a recruitment business, I started Market Partners with my good friend, Sacha Leagh-Murray.

The vision behind Market Partners was simple: If sales and marketing professionals recruited for sales and marketing roles, life would be easier. I wanted to create a recruitment agency that I would want to work with. I wanted to be a partner and an advocate, and to share in the risk and reward. Ultimately, I wanted to work with people and companies that I liked and respected and to help them grow to have the businesses, teams and careers that they wanted.

Over the next twelve years, we grew the business and in 2008 we merged the business to become a national entity called Carrera Partners. The following 4 years saw us build a good reputation in the market place with offices in Melbourne, Sydney and Brisbane. However, things just weren't right. As a leadership group, we wanted different things and wanted to take the business in different directions. Our purpose, passion and values were no longer aligned. I was finding it difficult to stay engaged and I no longer felt I was adding value. I didn't love my work anymore.

In November 2012, everything changed. I was given an amazing opportunity to travel to Uganda with not-for-profit, The Hunger Project, and I haven't looked back since. Up until this time in Uganda, I had always thought that I was a global citizen. I am educated, aware, caring and I thought I understood the complexities of issues such as hunger, poverty and injustice. I thought that I knew about the plight of the world's poorest and that I was contributing to a solution, after all, I sponsored two World Vision Kids, bought presents from Oxfam and gave donations to every charity event my friends and family participated in. However, it was not until this trip that I was confronted with what it was really like to have limited or no opportunities or choices. It opened my eyes and I saw the real impact of hunger, poverty and injustice.

Many of the things I saw, experienced and felt in Uganda are difficult to describe. What I did learn is that I had no right to complain about my life. I had no right to waste the opportunity I had to live the life I wanted. I am blessed to have been born into a life where I take the basics of food, warmth, education, healthcare, safety and even love, not just for granted, but as an entitlement. This is not the case for many around the world. I had been accepting all of this as a given, in the same way I was accepting that I had to stay in the business and job because it was 'the safe option'. Going to Uganda gave me the opportunity to question everything and to discover and appreciate that I had choices.

When I returned from Uganda, I had changed. It felt like I left Uganda with the heart, courage and determination of the women I had met there. These women were brave, they were resilient, they never complained. Why bother complaining when no-one was listening? They were purposeful and grateful for everything they had, they didn't wallow in thoughts about what they didn't have. So, I came back and viewed my life through a new lens. Instead of fearing risk and change because of what I might lose if I failed, I looked at my life through the lens of what I already had and how grateful I should be for it all. The thought of failure no longer scared me, instead I saw it as a blessing that I could make new choices, take different directions and to strive for more. Perhaps my most significant realisation was that life is very precious.

If I had been born in Uganda instead of Australia, there is no doubt that I would be dead. I had my second child at 40 years of age and there were complications. I barely survived the complications with the best medical attention money could buy, let alone if I was in Uganda or another of the world's poorest countries. I came back realising that every day is precious and needs to be lived. For so long I had been living for the future, "when I pay off the house I can do what I love", "when I get the kids through school, I can travel more", "when I get my superannuation to a point that I can retire comfortably, then I can think about helping others". I realised, I could be dead before I achieve any of those things so I needed to start living now.

I had changed and consequently, I changed everything. My business, my business partners, where I was going to send the kids to school and where we were living all changed. Though, I did keep my husband. It was after this life-altering experience that my life seemed to move into warp speed.

In January 2013, a few months after my return, we sat down as a family to discuss our commitment to The Hunger Project. The Hunger Project works on a Global Investor model. As a Global Investor you commit to a minimum donation or investment of $5,000 per year. With my 4 and 7-year-old sons and my husband we worked out what we had to change to find that $5,000. In the end it really wasn't that hard. We ate in a few extra nights a week, we had a few extra alcohol free days, my husband and I took lunch to work a few days a week and the kids agreed to one less present from us at Christmas and to help around the house for no pocket money. We have since found that our commitment to find $5,000 not only helps many around the wold but it has been of great benefit to our health and our family.

Shortly after my trip I was asked to join the Victorian Development Board the Hunger Project and within 12 months I was appointed Chair. When I was first approached about joining the board, of course I was flattered and excited, but I was also nervous. How was I going to fit it all in? I was running a business and raising a family, I was already so busy, how much more did I have left to give?

The funny thing is when you are passionate about something, it doesn't feel hard or like work and somehow you find the time. It just happens. Every time I attend a board meeting, or I meet someone who is inspired by the work we do at The Hunger Project and wants to help, I feel even more blessed, more energetic and more empowered to be better and do better. There is something incredibly uplifting and soul nourishing to do something for someone else, for the good of others, without any expectation of something in return.

On returning to Melbourne and my business, I realised I couldn't work the way I had been working. I was miserable and the business wasn't doing well. Not only was it soul destroying, there wasn't any financial reward. There was no reason to stay except for the fear of the unknown. Since 2012, I have been busy creating the life that I want. It has taken a lot of work, some risk and a few ups and downs but it has all been worth it. Let me tell you what I have done.

I got my business right

Just over six months after returning from Uganda, with the support of my amazing husband, my family and one of the business partners we demerged and started again. In a period of 5 weeks we rebranded ourselves and in June 2013, Chorus Executive was born.

After years of poor performance in its' previous form, since 2013 Chorus has had double digit growth, year on year, for the last 3 years. Our success has allowed us to launch 2 new service lines – coaching and personal branding and double the size of the team. We have won a number of awards including Top 5 Most Socially Engaged Recruitment Agencies in Australia and I was named a finalist in the 2015 Telstra Business Women's Awards.

I invested in learning

The world is changing fast and to stay relevant we have to change with it. I mentioned previously that Chorus Executive launched 2 new services – coaching and personal branding in 2013. Although, as an executive recruiter and head hunter, I have been offering career coaching for over 15 years, I had never completed an actual qualification. My philosophy has always been if you are going to do something, do it right, so in November 2013 I enrolled myself in a Post Graduate Diploma in Organisational Change and Executive Coaching. This 12-month course took me over 2 years to complete but I did it. I wanted to make sure that I could offer my clients the very best of me and now I am confident that I can.

I spent time with the people who are most important to me

In March of 2014 our entire family, including my mother, went to Las Vegas for our 10-year wedding anniversary. I wore my original wedding dress and we renewed our wedding vows with Elvis. We spent 5 weeks travelling around the US. We went to Disneyland and drove a campervan around the Grand Canyon, San Diego, San Francisco and LA. We did everything we wanted to do and it was amazing.

In the planning stages for this trip we had many people discouraging us with so many reasons why we shouldn't; "The exchange rate is too high", "It isn't the right time for business". "Wait until the kids are older", etc. etc. etc. I refused to continue only living my life for the future. We needed to live now. Of course we have to be sensible, but we also have to enjoy the present. 3 years on and my boys still talk about our incredible trip, the time they got to spend with us, but most importantly the time they spent with my mother – their grandmother. On our return my mother said, that the 5 weeks she spent with us travelling were amongst the best days of her life. Now, isn't that worth it?

I started to say, "yes", instead of finding reasons to say, "no".

We are presented with so many opportunities every day and yet I feel we are hardwired to say no without really understanding the reasons why. I started making a conscious effort to do this. I started saying, "yes", instead of finding reasons to say no.

This new approach had me saying, "yes", on a whim, to another 3 trips, all of which were to prove just as life-changing as my Uganda trip. In January 2015 I went to Antarctica. 6 months later, I was on Necker Island with Richard Branson and in January 2016 I went to the Amazon.

Of course I "shouldn't" have taken these trips. Everyone had an opinion – the cost, the time away from the business, my time away, from the family, what will your husband say? Thankfully I didn't listen because these trips have created opportunities I'd never have had, if I didn't say yes.

I have made lifelong friends and business associates from these trips, including one new business partner. I have found mentors who have helped me to grow my business and I was inspired with a new business idea. And, I drank Veuve in the pool with Richard Branson on Necker Island!

I wrote a book – we all have a book in us

As I said at the beginning of this chapter, I think everyone has an interesting and inspiring story. Most people are too scared to share it, not me. In February 2016, whilst in The Amazon, I launched my first book Hire Love – How to Hire Passionate People to Make Greater Profit. This book shares my story but also shares the Chorus Executive methodology of recruitment. Our fundamental belief is that people deserve to love their work and employers need their employees to love what they do if they are to achieve the business results they desire. During this process I was questioned as to why we would want to share our methodology and give away our secrets for success. My answer was simple. Organisations may not have access to our service or may not have the resources to work with us but they still need to hire the best people for their organisations. That's our vison at Chorus Executive, for everyone to love what they do as much as we do and to empower possibilities by creating powerful and profitable connections.

I took another big business risk

During one of my trips it dawned on me that the recruitment industry really hasn't changed in many years. Job boards such as seek.com.au in Australia and LinkedIn have created a more transparent and direct market place between job seekers and employers but the actual process has not changed much. This trip allowed me to get away from the day to day, I was able to be inspired by those around me as well as by my surroundings and I came up with the idea of creating an online version of what we do.

In 2016 we launched Peeplmatch.com, an on-demand candidate curation service where job seeker and employer matching is based on more than just skills and previous experience. This will be a revolution in recruitment.

We know, and there are thousands of research studies supporting this, that to be good at a job is more than just having the skills to do the job. You need to respect your manger and team, you have to feel aligned to the values and culture of the organisation, you need to believe that what you and what the business is doing, is important. Of course you also need to feel valued and rewarded and that you are adding value and making a difference with what you do. Current recruitment technology does not allow for this. Existing technology helps jobseekers and employers connect quickly or cheaply, but will not necessarily help you find the job that you, as a talented person, will love. That is the Peeplmatch vision – to work with job seekers to find jobs they will love, in organisations where they belong. We have only just launched so watch this space, there is more to come.

In 2012 I was running a business and a family, I thought I was busy and didn't have time. Clearly I was wrong. Look what can be done with a bit of prioritising and a belief that anything is possible. Look what you can achieve when you have a clear vision of the life you want.

It has taken me a long time to get me to this place. Like many people I just kept doing the same thing because it is what I thought I had to do, what I was meant to do. I had to get to the point where I was crying everyday as I arrived at work before I realised that it just wasn't worth it.

To create the life and career I have now, I had to pull everything apart about my old life, in particular, all my misconceptions about what I "should" or "could" do. I had to stop listening to others, who always had an opinion about what I should do, and start listening to myself. This does not mean that I don't ask for or take other people's advice; it just means that I no longer place more value on the opinions of others than on my own.

Here are my 10 Tips for Creating the Life You Want:

1.   Take Time Out -for you to understand and reconnect with yourself. This might be little breaks, or like me, it might be a life changing event like going to Uganda with The Hunger Project. Not only do we need the time but we deserve it. If people call you selfish for taking this time, smile graciously and ignore the comments. Once, when talking about my travels I was once told that I had a "long leash." I ignored the comment but when I told my husband he was really offended. "You are not a dog," was his response.

2.   Understand What Providing For Your Family Means - it is more than a house and paying the school fees. I find too many people live with a sense of duty and obligation not passion. I want my children to live passionate and happy lives, not lives of material comfort at the expense of self-actualisation and happiness. In 2013 when I decided to de-merge my business and start again, with all the financial and emotional risk this entailed, we spoke about this as a family. My husband's stance was, "If we have to sell the house, we will sell it. As long as you are happy and the kids are healthy, we will be fine." The children's response was, "Just be happy mummy, so you can play games with us again!" I will always prioritise the happiness of my family and myself over a new car or an overseas holiday.

3. Practise Appreciation - take time to appreciate all that you have to be grateful for. Funnily, we usually compare ourselves to those we think are "better" than us – better job, bigger house, smarter kids. If you consciously stop yourself doing this and start to see the world through a different lens, you will see that in fact, you are blessed already. Trust me, when I tell you there are more people who have less than you – less money, less health, less love and worse jobs than you.

4. Believe That You Have Choices - it is really easy to feel stuck and that you "have no choice". At the end of my time at Carrera Partners I felt stuck. I had to go away and take time out of the business to realise that the constraints, "being stuck", was only in my mind. We always have choices. We just have to be open to see them and then be brave enough to make a choice.

5. Surround Yourself With Amazing People - and weed out the rest. Just because you have been friends with someone since high school doesn't mean that they have to be in your life forever. If you walk away from someone feeling less energised or drained get them out of your life. I am not saying that you can only have happy friends. What I am saying is that those around you should support you, inspire you, challenge you and make you feel good when you are not feeling it and care. That is also your role as a friend. If you find that your relationship is one sided get out of it. It can be hard, but trust me when I say you will feel so much happier when you have the right people around you.

6. Be Smart With Your Resources - when you have resources you have choices. Your resources include:

a. Money - Don't spend more than you earn, it's as simple as that. If you are smart with your money this gives you the opportunity to take your dream job even if it is paying less than your current role, to start a business, go back to study or do anything else you are passionate about.

b. Time – Learn how to say no. Spend time with people you love and admire, doing things where you can learn and grow. The concept of FOMO (Fear of Missing Out) is outdated.

c.   Energy – Focus your attention and energy towards positive outcomes not negative thoughts. Dwelling on the negative and stewing over what is wrong just drains you more.

People – Use the strengths of the people around you. Ask them for help. Too many of us, believe that asking for help is a sign of weakness, a sign of failure. I think it is a sign of strength. Why struggle along alone, when you can ask those around you for help and create a better result.

7.   Be Brave - Stop using the words should, shouldn't and can't. Dare to dream and allow yourself to fail. Be open enough and brave enough to deconstruct your life, analyse it and recreate it. Sometimes you have to break it first before you can recreate it. Whenever I get scared about a decision I am reminded of something I read once; when a toddler learns to walk they fall over again and again and again. They have no concept that falling is actually failure or that they are "bad", "useless" or "unsuccessful". They just keep getting up until one day they walk. This is how I like to live my life. I have fallen down many times, but I have also run marathons! (Metaphorically speaking of course.)

8.   Give Without Expectation - it is amazing how good you feel when you actually give without expecting anything in return. Giving your time, money or even a compliment can have such a positive effect on the recipient. I find it is incredibly humbling to give with no expectations, just to be of help and assistance to some-one else and adding to someone's life, it helps keep me grounded. Expecting nothing back makes whatever you give a true gift, rather than an impersonal transaction.

9.   Learn To Celebrate Yourself - guess what? You are not perfect. And you know what? You don't have to be. Learn to accept yourself and love yourself. As I have got older it has been easier to do this. I now know what I am good at and probably more importantly, what I am not good at and I have finally accepted that I am not great at everything and never will be. Don't beat yourself up for all your failures and weaknesses instead; celebrate your strengths and successes.

168

10.	Believe That It Will Be OK In The End - some may call this optimism: I just think I am being practical. In the words of Oscar Wilde, "Everything is going to be fine in the end". If it's not fine, it's not the end."

Thank you for taking the time to read this chapter. I hope you got at least one insight from these words that could be beneficial to your life. If you have any questions or comments, please feel free to contact me on chris@chorus-executive.com.au

Christine Khor

About The Author

Christine Khor - founder of Chorus Executives. It's taken fifteen years of risk-taking, innovation, dizzying wins and dismal losses to make Christine Khor the successful business owner she is today. After a long and successful career working in product and marketing management for leading companies such as Kraft Foods and Simplot, she started her own specialist recruitment consultancy in 2000 with the very simple premise; that sales, marketing and communications people should recruit for sales, marketing and communication jobs.

Her business has undergone three major transformations to get to where it is today. The first was the birth of Market Partners, which survived a brief encounter with an embezzler, cornered the Melbourne market for sales and marketing professionals, grew in size and reputation and then considered expanding nationally. The expansion resulted in a merger with a Sydney based business and thus Carrera Partners was born. With offices in Melbourne, Sydney and Brisbane, the business was now nationally recognised, however after nearly five years, the relationships of the four directors became strained with differing visions for the future of the business. It provoked Christine to run away to Africa in order to gain perspective and bring meaning back into her life. She volunteered for The Hunger Project – a not for profit organisation that works to eradicate world hunger, and came back from Uganda a changed woman.

Her adventure lent her the strength to make the bold decision to demerge from Carrera Partners in 2012 – it was to be her biggest challenge yet, but resulted in the best payoff; the birth of Chorus Executive. A business that is wholeheartedly built on her values and vision; Chorus Executive is a holistic talent management company, providing recruitment, coaching and personal branding services to the sales, marketing and communications space. Her Melbourne staff remained with her and supported her through the transition.

A self-proclaimed change-junky, Christine lives for innovation and growth. She is a passionate speaker on career building, leadership, gender equality, work/life balance, small business start-ups and fulfilling your dreams.

At Chorus Executive, Christine specialises in coaching, mentoring, executive recruitment and organ-isation development. She is also the Chair of the Victorian Development Board of The Hunger Project. Christine recently adventured to Antarctica as part of The Unstoppables, travelled to Necker Island to join Richard Branson and a number of other prominent business leaders to discuss leadership, business and innovation, and was named a finalist in the Telstra Women's Business Awards for 2015.

Christine has also recently published her first book, Hire Love, to share her insight and knowledge on how to recruit passionate people to make greater profit and is the founder of Peeplmatch.com.

Building Relationships And Getting Free Press For Your Business

I have always loved building relationships with people, so it was no surprise and a complete joy when I combined my love of natural skin care with my love of serving people into a business. This business allows me to create friendship bonds in general and brand ambassadors in particular. Building customer relationships allows me to see that being nice matters. Being present matters, too. People want to be listened to and they want to have their problems solved. Whether it is a product or a service, they come to you for a reason and when you solve that problem and be kind and generous to them in the process, you create a forever customer and a relationship that really sticks. I believe it is the best part of small business and business in particular.

Reporters and writers are no different. They want to be treated with respect and they want to be thanked. Writers are artists and visionaries, and like you, they want to be recognized and appreciated for their work. They understand that you want publicity and that you want your name out there, but they also want to know that you are grateful for their help. Don't forget to thank them! This is such a key part of building solid relationships. Cultivating and maintaining these connections with the writers and reporters who use your work is one of the most important aspects of getting free publicity.

There are different ways to go about thanking writers and reporters. Tweet or comment to them when they post other stories. Publicize the story that you are quoted in all over social media. Have a page on your site dedicated to press, and show them it is there. Email or shout out a mention to the reporter once in a while, praising their work in general. Tag them in posts so they can see how much you are doing to promote the article and their writing.

Build your relationship with these writers and you will be remembered. Be the one they trust to always get the right quote or story. And the one they can count on. They will want to return to you in the future when they have a story need or a space to fill with something deeper. This builds your foundation, which in turn builds your brand. When you have a story to share with the public and a writer is the only avenue to get your story out, it is nice to have that type of relationship set in motion already.

Years ago, when I had another business, I had read a book, aptly titled, "Free Publicity, A TV Reporter Shares the Secrets of Getting Covered on the News" by Jeff Crilley, which outlined various ways to pitch stories and build relationships with writers and reporters. I never forgot it. I remember at the time when a Dallas Morning News reporter wrote about my then business, the phone started ringing with compliments and orders. It was unbelievably empowering. It was like getting a taste of the power of the press. More importantly, one of the key things I learned from that book and meeting with Jeff Crilley himself, was to always thank the reporter. He stressed over and over again how important it was to build confidence and trust with the reporters and writers, because then they will come back for more quotes or stories. I never forgot that wisdom.

What is the best way to make writers and reporters quote you? Make it as easy as possible! Ready to use quotes are the best, because they convey your message in your truest voice and spare the writer or reporter from the laborious task of rewriting what you give them (Trust me, this makes them very happy). Happy writers will be much more inclined to use your quote or written piece and, more importantly, they are more likely to remember you the next time they need an article or a quote on a similar topic.

I call them "write bites" and like memorable sound bites, they work. Entire paragraphs and quotes of mine have been used many times, even when I was just writing them to convey information.

Why is free publicity so vital to any business? The reason is simple. It is the best way to build character and credibility to your brand. It is the best way to show your audience the "Who" of what you are and not just the "What". When someone is about to make a purchase there are many factors involved. If your brand is competing with the attention of another, but your name is better known because you have been written about, the choice becomes clearer to the buyer. In this way it expands your influence, so whenever somebody writes about your business or includes you as an expert in your field, it is a credibility building block for future business. Marketing like this is a long term plan, but it is solid.

In a sense, free publicity is the best of both worlds—combining the reach of advertising with the rapport (and trustworthiness) of word-of-mouth communication. The secret to being heard in all the noise is deceptively simple: if you want your business to be found, you need to stand out from the competition. Getting published helps set you apart from the crowd; it is a way to publicize your brand without advertising. The more you are quoted as a source, the more you will be seen as the go-to person in your field.

PR tells your brand story. It builds confidence and familiarity. Publicity is an integral part of the overall sales process because it can be cost effective, cost efficient and very persuasive. An advertising campaign, on the other hand, also tells a story, but it is the company's "slick campaign" story. Free publicity is so wonderful because it adds a third person perspective, therefore another level to the consumers trust.

When I started my skin care business, ScrubzBody™ Natural Skin Care, in 2006, I had such limited funds that I needed to figure out creative ways to promote the product line and get exposure for the business. I remembered my meeting with Jeff Crilley and I just knew that free publicity was the answer to our marketing on a budget woes. I knew I just needed a push to get started.

First I looked up reporters online who wrote about skincare. It was time consuming, tedious and nothing much happened. I reached out to beauty bloggers, but I needed to send free product every time to even get a mention. Then I contacted a few writers with local newspapers. We got lucky and reached a business reporter. He ran an article about us, with a picture included, in our local newspaper. That one article generated so much buzz. It started our phone ringing and our online business humming, so I realized again how important getting free press was.

I needed a better, more efficient way, so I searched the topic. Help a Reporter Out (HARO) www.helpareporter.com, popped up first. I wasn't sure how to use the service, but I was intrigued. I signed up immediately and began receiving the emails three times a day. I was a little nervous to start because talking is more my strong point than writing, but I dove in and started writing pitches. They were clumsy at best, but I was learning. I took an online course about writing and my pitches got better. Finally, I got picked up to be part of a story. Then another. And another. I realized that writing the way a reporter wants to publish is key to being found and more importantly, having your answer be picked up and published. And I thanked them all. Since first starting with the HARO service I have been quoted or written about in over 100 publications on a wide variety of topics.

Many people understand the concept of free publicity but are nervous they won't be taken seriously. Or they feel they don't have enough expertise. Well, the cool thing is, if you have been working on your business or hobby for 6 months or more, you are more of an expert than someone just starting out. We all have those thoughts and fears! Putting yourself out there can be sweaty-palm scary. It can, however, also be the most empowering feeling—not just for your business, but also for your mind-set and your personal life. When you put forth your best information, it offers you a chance to hone your skills. It gives you the chance to try, try and try again. And the more you do it, the less scary it gets. Remember, there will always be someone who is behind you in the business world. They need help! *You have the guts, the goods, the gory and the glory to share what you have learned.* Wherever you are in your journey, you have great information others need. And if you have been in the game for a few years, well, you have all the hands-on experience you need to pass along your knowledge.

You can offer advice to aspiring entrepreneurs on what worked beyond your wildest dreams and what crashed and burned. You can give a testimony within your specific field, or offer encouragement to the broader small business community. I don't just know about skincare, but I know about running a small business. I know about online and brick and mortar. I know about charitable donations through the business. I know about inline skating and hiking Mt. Kilimanjaro on a dare from my brother. All of these business and life situations make for great quotes to writers and reporters looking for specific stories. No matter which topic I might speak about, if my words are picked up and quoted, so is a link to my business, and therefore, another way for people to find my company. Remember, it is not a quick return on investment, but it is a sticky one. Articles I was quoted in years ago are still providing a live link to my business.

Some of the best places to get free press are right in your hometown or area. Yes, being in the top magazines and newspapers is a tremendous compliment and will definitely give a boost to your brand; however, it's not going to happen on a regular basis. Local press keeps your name and your business brand in front of people's minds. Consider the local daily paper and the local weekly advertising paper that your town publishes. You read them, so remember that your neighbours and customers are reading these publications too. Nothing brings local traffic to your business like the local paper, especially if that paper's reference to your business is a news article and not a paid advertisement. Again, credibility building is a key to trust, which leads to a purchase. Isn't it great how that works?

Beauty bloggers, lifestyle magazine writers, business reporters and smaller business publications are other great ways to get your quotes published and your story heard. Anything printed online comes with a link to your business website and is another way for the search engines and people to find you. Some, like beauty bloggers, will ask for free product to review, however it is still much less expensive than traditional advertising. Make sure to vet the blogger. Visit their website and blog and make sure they speak well and present the same feel that you want for your business.

Another great benefit to pitching stories to writers and reporters is that it gives you a chance to hone your marketing skills in general. It gives you a chance to write with your heart and your mind about a particular topic that is near and dear to you. Whether or not a writer picks you up, this experience will propel your learning and growth. It is truly a win/win situation.

And the cool thing is you can always use the pitches you submitted for a future blog post! I have used so many of the pitches that I sent in but were not picked up as a catalyst for my own great stories. Sometimes, just having the idea and the outline (your pitch) is enough for you to write the best blog of your business.

Word of mouth is another free way to market your business and it adds the benefit of trust. People are much more likely to take a chance on your product when a colleague, friend or family member, rather than a paid ad, tells them to do so.

Friends and loyal customers will praise you and your products if you do right by them and give them great value. If you treat these new customers with respect and dignity, it makes the original brand ambassadors look good too. The return on word of mouth investment is huge. But it is usually a one on one situation; so building a profitable business based on word of mouth takes time.

Small business and the customer relationships I have built are the greatest business success I could ever imagine. I love the giving back to the community and I love knowing my customers. But, marketing for a small business can be the single most frustrating and challenging part of the business itself. That is where free publicity and the relationships you can build around it can make or break your business.

Roberta Perry

About The Author

After years of being selfless and taking care of everyone else's needs, (OK, that is my humble opinion, but work with me here) my skin was dry, itchy and irritated. In 2005, at 43, I finally realized that taking care of my skin and me was important. I discovered exfoliating products, but like the proverbial Goldilocks, none were completely satisfying my needs and wants. I headed for the kitchen and played like a "mad chemist" to create my own. I mixed up different combinations of botanical oils, which I had read were great for skin. I did even more extensive research and realized how lucky I was with the recipe I had created. I brought in my sister and we started ScrubzBody™, in 2006, in my home. The business quickly moved to a renovated garage and then we opened our first manufacturing/store front, in Bethpage, NY in 2011. We moved to a much larger space in 2014.

After all these years, we are proud of the fact that our products are still handcrafted with love in small batches. We host Make Your Own Scrubz™ parties for kids of all ages. We sell retail, private label and wholesale, with clients such as Whole Foods Markets and Wild by Nature. We donate to 6 charities, on a regular basis, with different scents of our products that give back, and we have co-hosted The Breast of Everything for the past 10 years.

Needing exposure for our business, but on a really tight budget, I turned to HARO (Help a Reporter Out) and started pitching to writers and reporters. Since 2010, I have been published and quoted in over 90 skin care and business articles, blogs and beauty magazines. I was a featured speaker on Indie Business Cruise 2016 about getting Free Publicity for your small business and my book, "The Power of Free Publicity, Using HARO (Help a Reporter Out) to Build Relationships and Get Press Without a PR Firm." was published in August 2016. I was a panellist for the LI Newsday Connect Small Business Seminar, I was a natural remedy segment guest of the Dr. Oz show, which aired on 10/24/14, as well as a food related segment which aired on 2/29/16. . I received the 2016 Nassau County Legislature Trailblazer award for my charity work. I am a proud member of Indie Business Network, American Made Matters, Bethpage Chamber of Commerce and Bethpage Kiwanis Club.

Point to Point Partners Press

The Power of Free Publicity, Using HARO (Help a Reporter Out) to Build Relationships and Get Free Press Without a PR Firm

http://www.pointtopointpartners.com/

poweroffreepublicity@gmail.com

Facebook: poweroffreepublicity

Twitter: @RobertaLPerry

Instagram: poweroffreepublicty

ScrubzBody ™ Natural Skin Care - https://scrubzbody.com

Finding Out What Being Successful Really Means

Running my own business was not my plan. Running my own mediation and conflict management business was certainly never my plan. When I graduated with my law degree, I thought I would be an employee solicitor for most of my working life. My aspirations were modest: I wanted a job I enjoyed and that I was good at, to help people through difficult times in their lives; to appear in court, present cases and get results for my clients; and to live a rich and fulfilling life outside of work. In 2012 I achieved all of that, but it was not making me feel happy or "successful". I felt at times that my life was passing me by while I did what was expected of me. I had worked hard to get where I was, but it wasn't right for me.

Outwardly I was on the "path to success", if success meant a secure job, higher than average salary and prospects to progress up the ranks of a law firm. I thought my success was bound up in my work, my status as a lawyer, and my financial standing. Since leaving that life and pursuing my own business I have learned that success has nothing to do with the job you hold, how much you earn, where you live or how often you eat out. Success is about who you are as a person and how you act towards others and towards yourself.

Becoming a lawyer had not been an easy path for me. In high school I decided that I wanted to study law at university and set my focus on getting into a "good" university. Years later I found some of my primary school mementos, which showed that even at the age of 5 when asked what I wanted to be when I grew up I had answered "a lawyer". I suspect it was because of the nice lawyer on *A Country Practice*. Like most kids I cycled through all sorts of other career choices including mounted police officer and mechanic (like Charlene in *Neighbours* – do you sense a theme here?). But by middle high school I had cycled back to becoming a lawyer.

When the university entrance scores were released I was aiming for 85+ to get in to law at my choice of university. I didn't think I would get the 90+ required for the top tier universities, but I was confident of getting in to one of my top two preferences. I opened my envelope and the bottom fell out of my world. 77. I had got a score of 77, nowhere near the score I needed; I felt like a complete failure and was inconsolable that first day. Soon after the score came out, the first round of university placement offers were made. All my preferences had been to study law combined with either arts or performing arts (my grand plan had been to study acting to enhance my court room skills), and to my surprise I was offered a spot; but it was for a university in Armidale, NSW. I didn't know anyone in Armidale; it was hours and hours away from home, and it snowed in the winter.

I did not want to spend the next 5 years of my life in Armidale. My preferred options were Canberra and Wollongong. Both cities were closer to my home town, and I had family in Wollongong, plus it is close to Sydney and is on the beach. I researched my options and I took a risk: I applied to study arts at the University of Wollongong, with a plan to earn high enough marks in my first year to transfer into law in the second year. My gamble paid off, and in hindsight, it was the best decision I could have made.

My birthday is 31st March, and I started school aged 4-turning-5, which meant that when I arrived for Orientation Week at UoW I was still 17 years old. This was going to be a year of fun and success. I enrolled in all the subjects I just knew I was going to love and excel in: French, Acting, Psychology, Music and a few law subjects on offer for the Commerce students, to get a head start on my plan to switch to law. By the end of the year I had learned so much, including that I was not enjoying studying French at tertiary levels and was not very good at it; I was not cut out for the 3 year Creative Arts (Acting) degree; and I love psychology.

My plan had been to transfer into an Arts/Law degree, majoring in psychology, but that required me to take other humanities subjects as well as psychology, and I hadn't found anything else I wanted to pursue at that level. Towards the end of my first year the university announced a new degree: Bachelor of Science majoring in Psychology. This degree was structured to allow students to focus purely on psychology subjects or combine them with other scientific disciplines. This was exactly what I wanted to do, study law and psychology and drop my other humanities subjects. I applied and was accepted. I was granted advanced standing for the psych and law subjects I had taken in first year, and was able to progress with my peers in the psychology stream. This was an option that had not existed when I was making my selections at the end of high school. Had I not taken the risk to start an arts degree and move into law from there, but instead accepted the offer to study arts/law at Armidale, who knows how things would have turned out.

Studying law was a mixed bag. Some subjects I enjoyed others I detested; I excelled in some, others were a real struggle. One summer a friend and I enrolled in Summer School with Southern Cross University. I don't remember how we found out about it, but the big appeal was that the 1 week intensive courses were held in Byron Bay. My mum, sister and some of our extended family were living in Ballina, about 30 minutes' drive from Byron, so I packed up my 1977 red Mini and, with my sister as co-driver, we road tripped from Wollongong to Ballina over 2 days.

My friend Rachel flew up and we had a great week in Byron studying the laws of war with a leading scholar in the field, who went on to become Director for International Law and Policy at the International Committee of the Red Cross (ICRC) in Geneva. I stayed on for an extra week for an intensive on psychology, psychiatry and the law, with a leading Melbourne barrister who has since been appointed as Queens Counsel, a Professorial Fellow in Law and Psychiatry at the University of Melbourne, and an Adjunct Professor of Law and Forensic Medicine at Monash University. At the time it was a chance to mix a beach side holiday with knocking over 2 subjects towards my law degree. The essay I wrote for the international laws of war subject became the foundation for my Honours Thesis: *From Charlemagne to Geneva – the History of the Laws of War*.

I graduated from my Bachelor of Laws (Honours)/Bachelor of Science (Psychology) in 2001 right around the time I landed my first full time job as a law clerk with a small firm in Helensburgh. For 12 months I drove the 30 minute commute each way to my job, and then spent evenings and weekends attending classes and completing assignments for my Graduate Diploma of Legal Practice (NSW having done away with articled clerks years earlier). I was finally admitted to practice in February 2003, 7 years after enrolling at UoW. In November that year I married Sam, who had supported me through my honours and graduate diploma, and remains my partner in all things.

Over the next 5 years I worked in 2 firms, learning a lot along the way both about the practice of law and the management of staff. In 2007 I was an Associate of my firm with an interesting and challenging portfolio of work. I was making budget and informally mentoring staff. I was being given the opportunity to take on more and more responsibility and to build a name for myself; but I wasn't happy and neither were others in the office. There has been instability in the firm with high turnover and a partner resigning to begin his own speciality practice. Tensions were high, morale was low, and junior staff came to me for mentoring, support and to voice their concerns. As a lawyer I was able to talk to the partners informally and let them know about the mood of the office.

On a personal level, I didn't see myself as a litigation lawyer forever, and had been considering other options. I was interested in learning more about frontline management (Sam had done a frontline management diploma as part of his job and it seemed a valuable set of tools for lawyer-managers, and something that was sorely missing from the industry), but with the previous redundancies still fresh in my mind, I began to think about other ways I could be a "fee earner" for my firm as well as a manager and struck upon the idea of being accredited as a mediator so I could be charged out by the firm, but not so weighed down in case work that I wouldn't be able to support and assist staff. And then I was promoted to Associate of the firm and the idea remained that, just an idea.

Roll around to 2012 and I was in another role that ticked all the boxes on my wish list, at least on paper. I was fit and slim, and I went to the gym regularly. I was in the best physical shape I had been since high school. I was living in Melbourne, the most liveable city in the world. I had a circle of friends who were also professionals making their way in the world. But I was once again – or perhaps still – feeling unsatisfied, unhappy and unsuccessful.

I was working as an in-house lawyer for a company that was undergoing a restructure and "culture change program". Morale was low as all around us colleagues' positions were being made redundant. At one stage our floor was only half occupied and later an entire floor was closed to save on overheads. A colleague and I used to commiserate "love the work, hate the workplace", but this had been the case for my last 3 jobs. Maybe the issue was me?

In May 2012 my uncle Bob died after years slowly dying as cancer ravaged his body. We had celebrated his birthday 6 months earlier with a huge family gathering, a bittersweet party that we all knew would be his last. My extended family is not large, and of all my aunts and uncles, I had been closest to him and his family. They were the ones living in Wollongong when I moved there for Uni, and they looked after me when I was a country kid lost in the bustling city (literally and figuratively).

I spend a summer living with them when I didn't want to leave my Wollongong friends and go back to a hometown that held little for me anymore. For a time Sam and I had lived around the corner from them, and we were regularly shared Sunday dinners and family gatherings. He was only 65 years old when he died; I was 34. I returned from his funeral in Wollongong and went back to work. The first conversation with my boss went along the lines of "I know you've been out of the office and have emails and things to catch up on, so instead of our usual 10am file review meeting, let's move it to 2pm so you have time to get caught up." No sympathy, no questions about how the funeral had been or the trip to Wollongong and back, not even how was I feeling, just business as usual. That was the first clue that the issue was not *entirely* me.

As the "culture change program" rolled on and more redundancies were announced, it became clear that the company's values no longer aligned with my own. We were being asked to do more with less, and when we raised concerns over ethical and professional standards, the non-lawyers on the executive dismissed our concerns. Lawyers in other departments were being made redundant and their roles given to non-lawyers who did not have the technical knowledge and skills required to do the job. There was a very real fear that our entire department would be cut and our work out-sourced to private firms.

I didn't want to stay in that job but I didn't want to start over again at another firm in another job. I felt like a failure and a fraud. I felt I had tried everything – working for privates firms, federal and state government, and in-house as a corporate lawyer - and that being a lawyer was just not for me. I had worked hard to get where I was and it was gut wrenching to think that I may have been on the 'wrong path' all along. I now know that there is no such thing as "the wrong path", but at the time it was daunting and I felt I had wasted a good portion of my life pursuing the wrong dream.

I started to think about other options. What else could I do? What else did I want to do? The idea of qualifying as a mediator bubbled back to the surface of my mind. I was working in-house in a role that would not allow me to be hired out as a mediator with fees paid to the company, so I asked to reduce my position from full time to part time, giving me a day or two to pursue outside interests. Obviously I expected to have my salary reduced pro rata. I pointed to working mums who had returned to the office part time after their maternity leave, and assured my manager that I would be available for court dates, mediations and other commitments that could not be rescheduled. My request was denied. I was told the company could not afford for me to be part time in addition to the working mums.

It all became too much for me. I felt unappreciated, unsupported and undervalued. In the course of a teary meeting with my manager she asked "are you resigning?" I looked at her and said "I think I am." I was coming up to my 35th birthday. My Uncle Bob had died at the age of 65. If I only had 30 years left on this planet, I was not going to spend them being miserable in a job that was not satisfying me, even though I had invested the last 17 years in to that career path.

In February 2013, 10 years and a day after my admission to practice, I said goodbye to my colleagues and walked away from my job as a lawyer. I wondered if I was walking away from the law altogether. One of my mottos in life is "never say never"; but on that day I was confident my mediation business would take off quickly and that I would soon be too busy and too wildly successful to think about returning to the practice of law.

Later that month I began my mediation accreditation course at Monash Uni and passed my exams a few months later. Mid 2013 I launched my business, with a website I had designed myself and business cards and stationary by a graphic designer. In September 2013 I received my National Mediator Accreditation. I was ready.

I now refer to 2013 as my "Gap Year". As well as studying for my mediation qualifications, I redoubled my efforts and completed the Diploma in Fashion Styling I had begun while still in my corporate job. I had signed up for a 6 month online self-paced course; 2 years later I held that diploma in my hand, and I am just as proud of it as I am of my Law and Science degrees. It represents a lot of time and effort, not only to complete the course work and assessments, but also a lot of work on myself. Since then I have learned the value of more formal and structured 'self-development' but at that time, I enjoyed the chance to reflect on what made me happy and what didn't; what I wanted from my work life and what I did not.

A friend was teaching at a local university, and needed tutors; so I taught sociology of health to first year nursing students for a year. I landed a job as store manager for a Sydney fashion designer opening her first Melbourne store (that job came to a shuddering halt when I suggested that she really ought to pay staff at award wages and pointed out her obligations under Fair Work; the next week I was restructured out of the job). And I tinkered away at the mediation business, certain that it was about to take off.

Learning about business

I sent out letters and emails letting people know I was now open for business and waited for the bookings to come pouring in; and waited; and waited. It turns out that "If you build it they will come" is not a sound business plan.

I did webinars and online courses, read articles and joined Facebook groups. I went along to networking events and when the Small Business Festival rolled around in August, I attended several seminars and workshops. I was still teaching, and eventually took on some casual customer service work to help pay the bills.

Even though I was doing everything as cheaply as possible – I won my first headshots package in a competition on Facebook - the business was costing me time, money and effort for little reward. I cringed inwardly every time someone asked me how the business was going. "Slowly but surely" I answered cheerily, but the truth was, it was not going. I had a few paying customers from time to time, but I was not attracting the right – or enough – people. I was still not "successful".

I now think of 2014 as a year of learning – learning about websites, search engine optimisation, marketing, advertising, book keeping, accounting, networking, referral relationships and sundry other things necessary when running your own business. Early in my legal career I had decided not to pursue my dream of becoming a barrister when I realised they essentially ran their own small business from top to bottom and, unlike on the British TV shows I had grown up watching, their clerks did not find them clients or handle their office administration. Ironically, here I was, 10 years later, learning all the things that had turned me off about life at the bar.

My First Mentor

Somewhere along the line I was feeling frustrated and sorry for myself, and complained to a brilliant networker I know that I was just not meeting the right people – being the kind of people who wanted to hire me. She suggested I join a particular Facebook Group, which I did. The group is run by a business mentor, speaker and author who provides support to women like me, wanting to build the business and life of their dreams but who are a bit stuck. I followed along the posts in the group and I took up some of the challenges and absorbed some of the lessons.

I went along to some workshops she ran in Melbourne, and then I joined an exclusive Mastermind group with 2 other business owners. For 6 months we met weekly, learning, growing and stretching ourselves. Out Mentor pushed us and challenged us. She helped me to uncover some underlying beliefs that were holding me back in business, and encouraged me to be more myself when promoting and acting in my business. Slowly I peeled away the lawyer layers.

Instead of the stiff photos in my suits I started appearing in more relaxed clothing that reflect my personality and style. I realised that one of my key strengths is my ability to explain complex and daunting legal concepts and procedure in plain English. It took about 4 months, but she eventually broke me of the "Hourly rate, pay after the work is done" mind-set (classic 6-minute-unit lawyer thinking) and helped me understand and embrace ways to package up my services and to get paid up front.

She got me to think about new and innovative ways of delivering my services so that, instead of sharing my knowledge and expertise 1-to-1 I could share it with many at the same time. She helped me turn my business around, from the inside out.

My path is my own

Of course, I now know I wasn't "on the wrong path", but rather, that some paths are more circuitous than others. The truth is, without my years studying and practicing law, I may never have fallen in love with mediation or ever branched out on my own. During my lawyering years I often threatened to "quit my job and sell dresses in a shop somewhere". Well I did that, and it wasn't any better.

What is "success" anyway? When I graduated from university I thought "success" was position, reputation and salary. When I launched my business, I defined "success" as a certain number of clients bringing a defined amount of money.

My goal was and remains to support Sam and myself so that he has the freedom to focus on his academic research and to work as, when and how he wants, not take jobs for purely financial reasons. It didn't happen straight away, and it hasn't happened yet, but I remain confident that it will happen, we will get there. But my financial goals are not the only measure of my success.

Now I define "success" differently. Success for me is a general level of happiness and contentment in my daily life. Success is sleeping well at night, knowing that tomorrow is a new day filled with new possibilities. Success is celebrating the small wins – a leader in my industry "liked" a photo or post I shared on Facebook; I helped someone get through a really difficult situation; I received a lovely testimonial or thank you email.

Success is being able to go to a movie at 10am on a Monday with my husband and an out of town friend, just because we can. Success is being able to set aside the day to day busyness of my business and to be there when my friends needs me – which I have been able to do twice this year, and will continue to do.

When the opportunity came up to write for this book on Successful Woman in Business a whisper of doubt said "you can't write a chapter on being successful in business because your business is still so new and not yet self-sufficient"; but that was not the point of this book. This book is about celebrating successful women, women who happen to be in business for themselves, and by any measure I am a successful woman.

My amazing husband and I have been married for over 12 years. Together we have moved house, jobs and states; we have travelled far and wide as well as explored our own backyard; we have faced triumph and tragedy together and I know that we have many more adventures ahead of us. We have some truly wonderful friends who are a constant source of strength and support, as are our families.

We live in inner city Melbourne with our pet rabbit who brings us joy and laughter every day. I have a balcony garden in which I grow food for us and our rabbit, and worm farms to help recycle some of our vegetable scraps and reduce our contribution to landfill. I make my own clothes, and mend, alter or recycle other garments into something new, further reducing my carbon footprint.

Friends trust me to care for their children, and permit me the honour of having some small hand in their growth and development. In return, I share my loves with those children: comic books, music, rabbits, fashion; and I share my values with them: feminism, equity, democracy, and self-determination, truth, honesty and integrity.

Running my own business was never my plan in life, but neither was being in a job without joy or satisfaction. My goal in life if to "be happy" and every day I take conscious steps to make that my reality. I may not be making a fortune in my business – yet – but I have contentment, satisfaction, ethical standards and values; I love and am loved; I have a positive impact in others' lives; and in all of that I am successful.

Rebecca Carroll-Bell

About The Author

Rebecca Carroll-Bell – The Everyday Mediator

Mediator, lawyer and conflict management specialist Rebecca Carroll-Bell helps people from all walks of life to eliminate drama and overcome conflict in their everyday lives. Using everyday language and techniques learned through her observation and study of human behaviour in and out of the court room, Rebecca brings a fresh approach to issues as diverse as family and divorce, workplace conflict and neighbourhood disputes.

A successful litigation lawyer for over 10 years, Rebecca brings her extensive negotiation skills and experience to conflict management and resolution situations. Described as "a great all-rounder – an attentive listener and a witty contributor" Rebecca's background in psychology and law allow her to nurture her clients when they need a little bit of emotional topping up, while keeping them accountable and calling them out on their junk.

For further information please contact: 0411770125

Rebecca@rcbmediationservices.com.au

Rebecca Carroll-Bell is The Everyday Mediator – passionate about managing, resolving and preventing conflict in everyday life: everydaymediator

Find Rebecca online at:

Website http://www.rcbmediationservices.com.au

LinkedIn https://au.linkedin.com/pub/rebecca-carroll-bell/25/580/1a

Facebook https://www.facebook.com/RCBMediationServices

Twitter https://twitter.com/RCBMediation

Google+ https://www.google.com/+RCBMediatorWestMelbourne

Instagram https://www.instagram.com/bec_cb/

Design the Lifestyle You Desire

As a working Mum, your business is just as important as your lifestyle. Yes you work hard logging long hours, meticulously balancing your books and leaving no loose ends. But if you launched a business for lifestyle reasons, and the majority of women do, you're not all work and no play. Maybe you like to cook, or travel, or just gab with the girls. Whatever keeps you smiling and sane is not going to take a back seat to business. In this section you'll find articles, blogs, and recommendations for ways to do something nice for yourself.

For me, it all started with the mission of creating a life I don't need a break from. Several years ago I wasn't in a good place but now, following a series of life changing events, I am (almost) living my dream. Life is full of ups and downs - but that's the beauty of it. It's just like the seasons; how would you appreciate the warmth of Summer without the cold from the Winter?

Autumn 1998 (I think), I visited my cousin who at that time lived in London. She was independent, very intelligent, lived in a gorgeous one bedroom flat and had an amazing career; she was my role model and still is! I decided that day that I wanted to become just like her; independent, intelligent, have my own flat in London and a great job.

Once I got back home; life happened, as it always does. Years went by, and I never went back to my dream of moving to London. In 2004, my daughter was born and I bought my first flat, not in London but in Norway. In 2007 my Mum passed away and I decided it was time to move on, so my daughter, Khushi, and I moved to London (!) in July 2008. The move was nothing like I had once dreamt of. It was full of pain and sorrow, but it was something I had to do at that time. We moved in to a beautiful one bedroom house. I had got a job as an Interior Designer at a Design Studio, but by the time I could work full-time, the company closed because of recession. Our life didn't start as I wanted, but I kept going.

Two years later (2010), I had got somewhat control over our life, but it was still a struggle. We moved in to our second home; a lovely two bedroom house. Slowly, we started settling down and life became 'normal'. In June 2012 I got a Restaurant Design Project who later hired me part-time as their Head of PR & Marketing. Life was good. Six months later, I was made redundant. I then (in February 2013) got a job as Head of PR & Marketing at an Estate Agent, I didn't enjoy it, but it paid the bills. After the 3 month trial period, I resigned and started working at a local College as Assistant of Marketing Director. Again, didn't enjoy the job, but I could work around my Khushi's school hours plus it paid the bills.

In January 2014 we moved to our Dream Home in the countryside of Hertfordshire. Six months later, I was made redundant (again), I was stressed out and fed up, but then decided to be self-employed and Build My Empire. And I have never looked back!

There were times where I kept asking 'WHY ME?' I just felt like no matter what I did, nothing worked out. I tried and I failed, I tried again and failed again. I kept focusing on what went wrong instead of everything that was going right. I am sure you have read this quote before? "Never regret anything because at one time it was exactly what you wanted."

I can so relate to this, and I am sure you can too. Once I started changing the way I thought, everything changed. Yes, once upon a time I did want to move to London, and I did! Maybe not the way I wanted, but definitely the way it was meant to be. Sometimes things we want do happen, but not always as we want to. And that is OK, embrace everything that is good, what's not so good, see it as a lesson, acknowledge it, learn from it and let it go - not for anyone else's sake, but for your own.

I was blessed to get another chance to start my life from scratch in London. From July 2008 until July 2012, my life was in 'slow motion', but since then my life has changed drastically - and I can proudly say that I did it all on my own:

1st runner-up, Women's Empowering Award, Nov 2012
Won Silver Website for My Unique Home, July 2013

\# Won the Inspirational Award in March 2014
\# Won Bronze Website Award for Vivacious Mum, April 2014
\# Won the Design & Creative Award at Asian Professional Awards, Nov 2014
\# Won Silver Website Award for Studio Kiran Singh, Jan 2015
\# Won Silver Website Award for Passion for Food, Jan 2015
\# Finalist 'Best in Creative Industries' category at the 3rd Annual British Indian Awards, April 2015
\# Won Silver Website Award for Design the Lifestyle YOU Desire! April 2015
\# Winner of Star Awards 2015
\# Finalist Network She Foundation International Women's Day 2016
\# Winner Bo-Concept One to Watch 2016
\# Finalist Hertfordshire Digital Awards 2016

Being a single mum can be pretty stressful and full of struggles at times. Single parents experience even more pressure to hold everything together and are particularly susceptible to burnout and the negative impacts of isolation and overwhelm.

My aim (especially since starting our life in the UK) has always been to Design a Life I don't want a break from, however I haven't been able to put this into reality since January 2014 - when we moved in to our new home.

This is different from trying to create a life that is one big vacation. I am aware of the hard work that will be involved and am happy to make sacrifices, however the constant focus remains that I want to enjoy my life so much, that I never utter the words I need a holiday ever again.

Below are my TOP 10 TIPS on how you can Design a Life you don't want a break from:
1. Long-term thinking your life and time has been worthwhile
2. Finding enjoyment in daily life and finding or creating work you love
3. Having a holiday mind-set, all of the time
4. Being prepared to work harder than we have ever worked to achieve this goal

5. Understand that money isn't the priority, happiness, contentment and fulfilment is
6. Create in ALL aspects of your life
7. Practice mindfulness and meditate daily
8. Turn your Home into a Haven; Live below your means, Feng Shui your Home and Life and Create a Beautiful, Healthy and Happy Home
9. Plan what your 'Ideal Day' would be like and make time to do things that make you HAPPY
10. Balancing adventure and reality - how to incorporate adventure into your daily life

I have broken this chapter into 5 topics; Inspiration and Goal Planning, Keep Learning & Start Growing, Things you need to do to successfully work from home, How to create a calm home office and Ways to find more hours in the day. I applied these ideas in my life, which not only boosted my business but most importantly I learned how to keep a healthy family and work balance as it's crucial (especially being a single Mum in my case.) So...with no further ado, let's get started!

Vision, Inspiration & Goal Board

I start my year (like many others) with the very famous 'New Year's Resolution List', BUT I don't just write it down in a notebook or journal and forget about it. I create a (rather big) vision board. What's a Vision board you ask? It's a collage of words/quotes and images, which make you, feel positive and empowered, inspiring you to accomplish the dreams you have placed on it reminding you of your true passions and desires. By seeing your goals on a vision board, will help you to identify your vision and give it clarity, reinforce your daily affirmations and keep your attention on your intentions.

My vision board changes every month – as in I update my goals, quotes, inspirational images and most importantly the highlights and achievement of the month – which daily reminds me of being grateful and see how much I have achieved. I am sure you agree with me when I say that in the hustle and bustle of life we keep striving for more and more without realising how far we have come.

Keep Learning & Start Growing

From the moment we are born to the moment we die we never stop learning. Whilst we may not always 'learn' in the context of a formal classroom setting, or even though we may not be aware that we are consciously learning new things, every experience we have will teach us something.

For those who choose to embark upon a program of personal development or self-growth, they have often taken the decision based upon their perceived or actual need to change something about themselves or their lives that isn't working for them. This process often results in them finding themselves on a road leading to personal enlightenment. Their 'new' life will seem so much better than what they would often refer to as their "previous existence" and, for those people in particular, their new zest for life will result in a lifelong learning experience which is aimed at leading them to personal fulfilment.

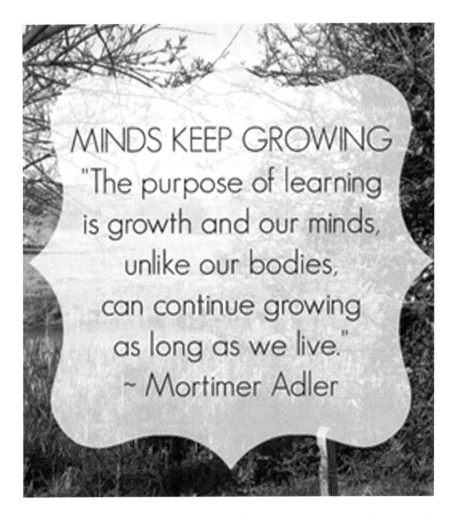

I love learning, expanding my knowledge, continue developing myself by reading, listening to podcast, doing courses, attending events - the list in never-ending. I have for about a year wanted to enrol onto a personal development course - something that can help me continue my journey of discovering my authentic self, something that can guide me to understand and connect with life on a deeper level and to understand and be a better listener.

So within the last 6 months I have done Diploma in Life Coaching (my 2nd Life Coaching qualification), Mindfulness, Self-Confidence, Law of Attraction and

Counselling Skills. Next on my list are NLP Practitioner, Mobile Phone Photography and Social Media.

As these are all long-distance learning courses, I can do them in my own time-frame - I have given myself a deadline to submitting all the assignments by end of August! I'm super-excited about this and have scheduled in a 2-3 hours daily (mostly in the morning, after the school run and my morning walk) to study. These courses are perfect for continuing my professional development - to become a better Life & Mindfulness Coach along with the bonus of having Counselling Skills.

If I've got the weather on my side, my office is of course outside - with my pink laptop and a cup of divine Earl Grey Tea. There's nothing more inspiring and energising sitting outdoors and work / study to the sound of birds tweeting, the river running and piano music playing on low in the background.

I take a 10 minute break after each 50 minute working / study session. I will lie down in my hammock doing a quick guided meditation - I've downloaded a few guided meditation apps from Mindifi which I quite enjoy.

10 Things You Need To Do To Successfully Work From Home

You've done it! Congratulations! You've finally escaped the clutches of everything you've been secretly plotting against for way too long. The grumpy boss. That sardine-like commute. The burning smell of the world's worst instant coffee drifting from the kitchen. Office politics. Work that didn't really matter to you.

But somehow it's 6pm already. Another day has drifted past in a flash. Your feet are still bare because you didn't feel the need to put socks on today. You're in familiar surroundings and you don't have to spend an hour getting home, but what have you really achieved?
Here are ten things you need to do in order to work from home like a boss.

1. Give yourself routine

If working from home is new to you this is going to take a little while to adapt, but the sooner you set parameters for the working day the better. Know where you're going to work: this might change from morning to evening depending on how light shifts around your home office – let's call it a hoffice. Make sure you're at the desk by a set time and embrace getting up early, this is ok if you're the one who decides you have to. Yep, you can play the snooze game, but boy it feels amazing to have nailed a ton of work before 10am.

Map your day according to how you think you'll feel if you complete a certain set of challenges and let your measure of success revolve around tasks, not time.

2. Get up, shower, put clothes on

Don't work from bed. Beds are for sleeping and other kinds of magic, let them be precious and special in their purpose. Wash the night away before doing anything. Getting straight to work because you can, doesn't mean you're on fire, because after a while you're going to start itching. A sweaty homeworker is a silently disgruntled homeworker.

Blast your head with water, get fresh and don't forget that you're still a human even if you don't have to spend your day with others. Now, put some clothes on. Yes, there's a temptation to wander around in the nude and make phone calls, because you can. But don't. Wear what you like as long as it's not pyjamas, but wear something. Now, you're ready to get started...

3. Focus: read, don't type over meals

This is about honing your focus and ability to juggle different actions. If one of your hands is holding a spoon or a fork or a knife or a jar or a mug or a piece of fruit, you simply can't type properly. Stop trying to do everything at once, we're trying to make you into the most efficient working-from-home-beast possible. Open up a couple of blogs, articles or news pieces and read – this is stretching for your brain before you start doing cartwheels towards your own work.

4. Prioritise: Write a To Do list, yesterday...

Thinking 'what do I do now?' is the first step to potential boredom, and boredom kills dreams. Don't be a dream killer.

To Do lists sound like they were invented by a cruel master, but they're the key to self-motivation. This is your list and the summation of the day you've decided you'd like to have. Take ten minutes before you sleep every night to make the next day's list— give yourself something to be excited about. Prioritise no more than three biggish tasks, and don't be afraid to have a secondary list on a different page with things that need to be done, but not necessarily tomorrow.

Know what you have to achieve and give yourself a timeframe to realistically do it well.

5. Set the musical mood

Your working environment is key. Be in a room with lots of light. Move your working space and direction around until you're happy. Don't have your back to the room, face it.

Working in silence is a distraction so get Spotify premium (other services are available) and find a Focus playlist. Vivaldi is scientifically proven to aid concentration but most classical music is perfect to start your working day (this isn't about musical preference, it's just clever ambience). If you're writing don't choose tunes with lyrics, you'll only be tempted to sing along.

6. Destroy distraction

This is the difference between a good day and a bad day. Put your phone out of reach when you're working or at the very least put it on Airplane Mode. A WhatsApp notification is distraction. So is a new match on Tinder. Or a new Tweet or Instagram or Facebook or advert or reminder. Stop it!

Save direct messages for break time and give your focus a chance to be relentless. Struggling not to automatically click onto Facebook to see how many likes that video of a kitesurfing squirrel has now? There are a couple of self-control apps that will physically stop pages like Facebook opening during the times you choose.

Basically, if anything during the day takes your eyes off the prize at any given moment make sure that you find a way to stop it happening in the future.

7. Work on, work off
If you're running for a whole day with no stops to refuel, drink or rest, the person who chooses to run for only 45 minutes each hour will go further than you. Be a tortoise and rest your way to victory.

There are a bunch of ways to do this, but here's a starter: at the beginning of each work session set your phone timer to go off in 50 minutes. As soon as it beeps, stop working for ten minutes. Stand up, move around, drink water, and breathe. Try not to look at a screen but if you must, this is your window to check and reply to WhatsApp. Then after ten minutes set the timer, and get going again. Three or four hour-long sessions might feel productive, but you'll do more if you have multiple rests in that period. Be smart, not relentless.

8. Be email clever...
For years I had a thing: my inbox is my To Do list – my work isn't over unless it's empty. At heart, this meant I got things done, but there was a downside because I never closed it. If you're an inbox Nazi just breathe. Every email you send out is potentially asking for another one back and if you're in the swing of things you could spend all day on email without time for rest. A productive day is not a day spent online. An open email inbox is a destructive taunt and temptation, and the moment I tried a new technique I started getting more successful.

So now I only check email at certain times. The first window is 10-10:30am, which gives me two hours on a typical work day to write, create and not get waylaid. Half an hour is enough time to reply to urgent messages and to get a feel for other work or opportunities, but don't get sucked in. If there are pressing issues another half hour of email in the early afternoon is ok, but I save the bulk of my email clearing until after the working day for most people who email me is over. This way they're not going to be replying immediately, letting me get on with other stuff.

If you have a remote team and use WhatsApp, slack or a similar app to communicate, try not to let it take over your life. Treat it like email, or only engage with it every hour.

9. Group similar activities
Group your skypes, conference calls and in-person coffee meetings. Block out a couple of mornings or afternoons each week for chats and leave the rest free for unbounded, undisturbed work.

10. Get Outside
Don't forget to exercise. You don't get it done on your bike commute anymore and now that you're in charge of your own destiny there might be a feeling that if you stop working you're harming your chances of success. Here's a newsflash: getting pale and porky in your home office is just going to make you tired and, in the long run, ill. Get some vitamin D, ride a bike, go read on a park bench, smell fresh air. Spend at least one day a week out and about. Go and see real people and get inspired by conversation.

For all the freedoms of working from home, if you don't make it count that freedom might one day have to get shelved. It doesn't have to be this way. Be good to yourself, work smart, learn as well as do and base it all on creating a habit to get things done.

If you try and cook an elephant every meal, you'll end up never eating* so break down the big stuff into smaller chunks and tick off hundreds of little tasks a day. Build momentum, be nothing but a doer and when you finally get to bed at the end of the day, make sure that you've made it count.

How To Create A Calm Home Office

Your kids are clamouring for attention. Your husband asks if you can make a quick pit stop at the dry cleaners for him, and the dog keeps whimpering to be let out. Working from home sure can feel like a balancing act sometimes. Here's how to bring some Zen back into your life and create a calm home office, too.

Clear the clutter

Whether you have neatly stacked piles of paper everywhere or it's been six months since you last saw the surface of your desk, clutter can be a mood killer. Not only does it zap energy, but it can also cause you to feel frustrated, disorganized, and overwhelmed. Steer your way to a cleaner office by de-cluttering your space.

To get to the bottom of the clutter, work in sections. You can start with your desk first by removing all the items from it, and then deciding what needs to be kept, tossed, or donated. Do this for all areas of your home office - including your kids' toys that have magically made their way into your space - and you'll have a neater home office in no time.

Pick your paint

The walls of your office are a bright lemon yellow. Is it no wonder that you feel stressed every time you walk into your space? Colours can help bring energy into a space and most definitely impact your overall mood. To optimize your productivity - and avoid an anxiety attack each and every time you sit down to work in your home office - try more calming, soothing colours. For example, pale greens, beiges, and blues can bring out your softer side and calm you down.

Get some fresh air

If you're working in a home office that has stagnant air, you'll wind up feeling pretty stagnant and unhappy, too. So if you have a window in your space, keep it open! The fresh air will do wonders for your productivity. If your space is sans windows, you can always keep the air and **ideas circulating by using a fan.**

Another way you can bring the outdoors in is to have a house-plant sitting on your desk. Some household plants can purify indoor air and even remove harmful household toxins, too! Some of these plants include Aloe Vera, Boston Fern, English Ivy, and the Peace Lily, among many others. In addition to boosting your O2, having the added boost of green from your plant can be calming, too.

Sure, working from home is wonderful in so many ways, but there are stress-ors to deal with, too. Follow these tips, and you'll be saying "Om" in your home office in no time!

10 Ways To Find More Hours In Your Day

We all wish we had just a bit more time. Just think what you could do with an extra hour or two each day: you could finally stick to an exercise routine, or spring-clean the house, or write your novel, or learn the guitar, or get a new qualification. It can't magically make all your days 25 hours long. But it can help you find more hours in your day for the things that really matter. The below tips are both for those who work outside and for those who works from home.

1. **Get Out of Bed Earlier**

If you normally get up at 7.30am, try getting up at 7am. That half-hour might not sound like much -- but it could be time that you use to meditate, to exercise, to read that book you've been meaning to finish, or simply to get your day off to a calm and organized start.

The first hour or half-hour of the day is often a great chance to work on something important, before other demands crowd in on you. And, if you need your beauty sleep? Just get to bed half an hour earlier.

2. **Use Your Commute Productively**

How much time do you spend commuting every week? Unless you work from home, you've probably got at least a couple of hours each week when you're traveling between your home and your workplace.

Use your commuting time for something useful. If you drive, you could listen to audio books. If you take the bus or train, you could read a book rather than grabbing a free newspaper. And if your workplace is quite close by, you could try walking or cycling to work -- this builds exercise into the natural rhythm of your day.

3. **Tackle the Important Tasks First**

Once you get to work, take a few minutes to prioritise your tasks. Get the *important* ones done first (not the easy ones, or even the urgent ones). You can afford to spend at least an hour working on big, important tasks rather than on all those little urgent ones.

If you work like this, you'll usually save time: the urgent tasks will still get done, and you won't spend hours procrastinating over the important ones.

4. Don't Check Email So Often

Your colleagues and clients can wait for a few hours -- or even a day or two -- for you to reply to their emails. If there's something truly urgent, they'll pick up the phone.

Keep your inbox closed when you're working, and only open it when you're ready to spend 30 minutes or so dealing with emails. It's much more efficient to batch-process your emails than to keep popping in and out of your inbox to deal with individual ones.

5. Reduce Interruptions

If colleagues have a habit of hanging around your desk to chat, or if the phone is constantly ringing, you might find that it takes you half the day to finish a simple task like writing a letter. Constant interruptions don't just eat up time -- they also break your concentration.

When you've got a big task to focus on, let your calls go to voicemail. If you have an office door, close it. If you work in a cubicle, wear headphones: having them on makes it less likely that people will try to strike up a conversation (you don't have to listen to anything through them).

6. Stay Focused on Your Work

You might have heard the saying "procrastination is the thief of time. When you want more hours in the day, procrastination can be a real problem. A few minutes chatting, browsing the web, updating your Facebook status, and so on, can easily turn into hours of wasted time over the course of a day.

When you're working, work. If your concentration is slipping, take a proper break: go and get a glass of water, or stretch your legs a bit. And if you're facing a difficult task, try breaking it into small steps or stages so that it's easier to tackle.

7. Go Home on Time

If you're supposed to finish work at 4pm, but you never make it out of the office door until 6pm at the earlier, then it's no wonder you don't have enough hours in the day.

In some jobs, it is difficult to get away on time (if all your colleagues work late, you might feel obliged to do the same). But if you're staying because you only ever seem to get any work done in a mad dash at the end of the day, then your working habits need to change.

8. Delegate Some Chores

Perhaps you seem to be the only person in your household who's capable of un-stacking the dishwasher or ironing the clothes. If your evenings get taken up with a long list of chores, see whether you can delegate some of those.

Your partner, housemates, or kids can pitch in and help out. Even if you just free up 20 or 30 minutes every evening, you'll have a bit of extra time to spend on something important to you.

9. Eat Dinner at Home

Although going out for dinner might seem like it saves time (after all, you don't have to cook) – you've got the time cost of travelling to the restaurant, ordering the food, waiting for it to arrive, paying the bill ... and it might well be faster just to cook and eat at home.

If you don't have much time to cook during the week, try making extra portions at the weekend so that you can freeze some. That way, you've got an almost-instant meal (and one that's probably healthier and cheaper than a restaurant meal, too).

10. Limit Your TV Watching

If you put the TV on as soon as you get in from work, it's easy to end up spending hours slumped on the sofa.

Instead of watching whatever happens to be showing, try watching just one or two programs each night.

You might also want to have at least a couple of TV-free evenings; a great chance to read a good book, or to work on a project around the house.

Well...this is it for now. I hope you found my tips and ideas useful and helpful and that once you apply them in your life, you will notice a big difference. Just remember, being a successful business woman isn't only about business, it's all about YOU!

You need to put yourself and your needs first; practice self-love and self-care daily, do at least 3 things every day that will make YOU happy.

Listen to your intuition – your inner wisdom, write down 3 things you're grateful every evening before you go to bed, treat yourself daily; wear your favourite perfume, your favourite lingerie, put on that bright red lipstick you've kept for special occasions – every day is a special occasion!

Go for a walk; see the beautiful nature, feel the gentle breeze touching your skin. Eat cake or chocolate. LIVE your life!

Plan your days, weeks, months, quarters and year. Start with writing your top 5 goals for the year, and then break them down to small steps over the coming months, weeks and days.

Believe in yourself, set realistic goals – enjoy the journey, not just the end result.

Trust Your Journey!

Kiran Singh

About The Author

I am a Single Mum (by choice) and a Multi-Award Winning Entrepreneur. I am a Life Coach at Design the Lifestyle YOU Desire, an Author and Residential & Hospitality Interior Designer at STUDIO KIRAN SINGH, Founder and Editor-in-Chief of Vivacious Mum, My Unique Home and Passion for Food. I run a local support group for single parent's through Gingerbread. I am an Expert at The Women's Room and HerSay Expert.

My mission is to help mums envision, create & design the life they really want. My vision is that my message will remind you daily to be grateful for what you have but mindful of what you can become. Life's challenges come in all sizes, shapes and colours. You already possess the inner strength to deal with any situation. I specialise in Life Coaching, Mindfulness Coaching and Law of Attraction Coaching, Single Parent Coaching and 'Business Start-up' Coaching.

Design the Lifestyle YOU Desire's statement: To guide, empower and encourage women to honour their inner strength and celebrate their unique, personal path through life.

I believe in my saying; "Each and every step leads you to the next, and every person in your life leads you to the next as well... look how far you have come, not how far you have to go... you are not who you were... you are who you've become. Stay positive, stay determined, and you will keep being a better version of you."

You can connect with me here:

Website: www.designthelifestyleyoudesire.com

Facebook: https://www.facebook.com/DesignTheLifestyleYouDesire/

Twitter: https://twitter.com/kiransingh

Pinterest: https://uk.pinterest.com/kiran_singh_77/design-the-lifestyle-you-desire/

Instagram: https://www.instagram.com/studiokiransingh/

Google+: https://plus.google.com/u/0/b/103982148418757103351/+DesignthelifestyleyoudesireDTLYD

Kiran Singh, Multi-Award Winning Entrepreneur, Life Coach & Author

MCMA (Member of The Complementary Medical Association)

IAHT (Member of The International Alliance of Holistic Therapists)

IANPLC (Member of The International Association of Neuro Linguistic Programming and Coaching)

4 Lessons on How to Increase Success Rates for Any Start-up

How do you define success? Everyone has his or her definition of success. In my opinion, success is to have the freedom to achieve your dreams and most importantly, to be able to make life better for others.

I'm an entrepreneur who started her own first IT business at the age of 29. Prior to my own start-up, I was an employee like many others too. So you might ask, why did I decide to start my own business? The first reason is very simple. I love money (who doesn't?) and I do not want to be poor again. Incidentally, I had a taste of poverty when I was younger and had to suffer under financial loans in order to achieve my basic education. Although money cannot buy everything especially happiness, but it gives you the ability to afford some things in life that can bring some short-term happiness when you do not have everything. It is what you do with the money that is important. For example, we were too poor to travel when we were younger, so the ability to take my family on holidays to create plenty of memories and experiences is money well spent.

Second reason - there is this burning passion inside me for technology. I enjoy and get excited with the changes that technology brings and I love to see how it can impact the way people live and work. Many successful people will tell you that you need to be passionate about something before you can start your business. I would say that this is only half true. Research and make sure your passion is in demand too, then jump into it and bring your passion with you. The last thing you want is to be passionate about something for your whole life, but die poor.

Let me give you an example. I am a qualified Pilates instructor. I took up the certification when I was still employed full time. I strongly believe in the benefits of Pilates and feel that there will be a demand for it. And so, I wanted to start a Pilates business, but at that point of time, not many people in Singapore had heard about Pilates and there was low demand for it. I was teaching it on a freelance basis for a while at some local gyms but eventually it died down. My savings would have gone down the drain and I might have landed myself in debt if I had made that decision back then to start a studio. I did not have the capital to wait for the market to mature. With twenty thousand dollars in savings from eight years of employment, I took the bait and started Nucleo Consulting, an IT consulting company. IT has always been my passion from a very young age and it is always in demand.

Last but not least, I believe that I can make life better for others and also play my part to be a responsible human being on Mother Earth. In Nucleo Consulting, I love to put together solutions that can help SME businesses be more productive. Solutions that will increase their profit by making their staff more productive. We also assist our clients to dispose of their e-waste so that our clients can be more environment-friendly. On a company level, Nucleo Consulting is also a sponsor for ACRES (Animal Concerns Research & Education Society), a non-profit charity organization in Singapore that focuses on helping wildlife. Personally, I support a couple of charity organisations that focus on children and low-income families. Giving back to society is equally as important to me as earning money because I was once helped by others and feel I should pass on the kindness.

Entrepreneurship can be for everyone, but there is no easy way to go about it. It is pure hard work and positive mind-set. So is passion alone enough? Actually, no. It requires dedication and perseverance. I have written a book called *"Obstinacy Power"* which talks about my 6-step strategy for achieving determination, not just for starting up business, but also for every goal that you have in your life. That book contains more in depth detail on how I managed to use the same strategy to achieve my goals in my life - from winning a car in an endurance challenge, to my business start-ups, to finishing a full marathon and my latest goal, to compete and win Latin dance competitions. But for now, I want to share with you a few lessons that I have learnt after running a couple of businesses.

Lesson 1: Find a Partner

Depending on your business nature, you might want to find some like-minded people to partner up to start a business. I would say that the best is to keep the number as small as possible for a start-up. Part of the reason is because the initial profit would be little and the small pie has to be shared among the partners. Some people will not have the patience and faith in the business and the chances of falling out is higher when more people are involved. Two to three would be a good number. The more people you have, the more different opinions you will hear and so you might have more arguments and disagreements too.

On a positive side, you may also get more new ideas, as there are more brains to brainstorm together. You have to recognize the fact that you can't always do everything alone, you will need to share the pie because it helps to shorten the path to success if all partners have the same mind-set. Can friends or your spouse be your business partner? Yes, if you know this person very well and can trust this person. I have friends who say that it is best when your spouse is your business partner as you can be 100% assured that you can trust this person. It also brings more motivation to the marriage and more topics for discussion as well. But both parties have to be very objective especially in arguments. Constructive arguments are good.

Lesson 2: Choose the Right Partner, just like in Marriage

I think this is one of the most critical parts of the start-up. Partners must have the same vision and be able to stand together during good and bad times. It is always better to get a stronger and more experienced partner in every kind of partnerships in life. You will get to learn from each other and as long as both are focused on the objective and able to have constructive arguments, the partnership will be successful. It would be the best if you can complement each other's skill set too, so that you can minimise the external resources needed during a start-up. Many times businesses fail due to partnership arguments, even though they might have great ideas or products. In any partnerships/relationships in life, you have to be truthful to yourself. Be committed to your objective/goal and communicate clearly to your partner. I think that is the key to success for any form of relationship, be it business, marriage or dance partnership. Otherwise, you will just be wasting everyone's time and your life away. So choose wisely.

Don't get overly excited when you meet someone who shares the same idea as you. Talk openly and have a few meetings, understand how each other behaves when facing tough situations. Establish whether that person will fight or flight, see how long he/she already had this idea lingering in their mind and their financial backing if both of you need to pool resources to start up. Don't take too long to discuss. Put it into action and make sure the other partner is also as committed as you are. Make sure your potential partner is not a procrastinator because it will result in the failure of the business.

Lesson 3: Learn to Outsource or Delegate

As a start-up, resource is always a challenge. There were plenty of challenges I encountered when I first started out on my own and I had to learn everything on the job. There is no right or wrong way to run a business. The business model can change and should evolve over time due to the changing demand of the market. You could easily get burnt out because there is so much to learn and a lot to do. I was working sixteen hours a day when my business just started. It was for a period of almost a year. But you should learn to delegate and outsource certain parts of the business so that you can focus on the important ones i.e. bringing in sales to pay the bills. The first thing that I outsourced was accounting. Although I did basic accounting, I figured that I should spend my time bringing in more sales and doing customer servicing instead of trying to tally my numbers and risk getting the wrong figures for a tax submission. I realised that there are many professional accounting firms that can assist with such needs and they will make sure that our company meets the relevant regulations and submit our accounts on time to avoid any penalty. This gives me a peace of mind and I can focus on what I need to do. Don't be penny smart but pound-foolish. Certain money needs to be spent, and this is one of the typical ones.

Another example that I can quote was when I was hiring my first staff member. I did the recruitment process myself and it took me weeks to vet through resumes to try to find someone. But I wasn't able to find the right person for the job. Eventually, I went to a recruitment agency, which found me someone that fits the culture and the job. I was trying to save on the commission but I realized that I should not save that money because these recruiters had more experience in judging the right candidate for me. I was also assured that they had gone through a series of phone interviews and spoken to them prior to sending them to me for an interview. That saved plenty of time. Always remember, you can use money to buy some resources if needed, especially when time is critical in a start-up and you really can't do everything yourself.

Lesson 4: Get a Mentor

Getting a mentor is one of the best ways to save you time and increase your chance of success. You can avoid banging your head against the wall and making the same mistakes that other people have made before. It also allows you to gain confidence in building your business too. It may not be easy for you to find a mentor. There are many ways to find a mentor and it is not about going up to a stranger and just asking them to be your mentor. Observe their work, they may or may not need to have a personal connection with you. Ideally, it is best to be able to communicate regularly with your mentor. Your mentor doesn't have to be someone famous, but must have already achieved what you want to do, for example, a successful million-dollar business owner that has presence in Southeast Asia.

Have an open mind and a learning attitude and attend networking sessions to make connections with people. Communicating with people is an art and it is an essential skill that you need if you really want to be successful in life. You should not expect your mentor to always check on you and your progress. So you have to be self-motivated. Imagine if you are the one mentoring someone, you would not like it if you had to babysit that person. After all, it is your own success in life and not theirs.

I have been very lucky to meet a few mentors during the course of my businesses. All of them gave me different advices during different stages of my businesses and I am very thankful for that. These golden words remain in my head and are my source of motivation when I meet an obstacle. Here are some words of advice from 2 successful women in business that I would like to share with you.

One of my mentors, Ms Mathilda Koh, the founder and CEO of Bioskin Holdings Pte Ltd, a beauty and wellness company, told me this before – to be an entrepreneur, you must have these 5 powers : The power of courage, determination, endurance, energy and strive. She started her company Bioskin at the age of 22 and went through a few economic crises. Her company is now a renowned leader in the beauty industry and staying competitive has definitely not been an easy feat.

The 5 Powers:

1. Courage - To take the step to move the business in the direction that you want to.
2. Determination - To push through obstacles in your way.
3. Endurance – To endure any setbacks and not let it get your spirit down.
4. Energy – To be able to run everything all on your own when needed.
5. Strive - To fight for your goals.

Another mentor of mine, Ms Foo Lai Chan, Managing Director of IFBC, a US-listed food company, once told me that no matter what I do, I must know my market and do my research well. It is extremely important that I know the products and services that I am selling and customers must get the value of what we are selling.

Only then can you turn them into loyal customers. Ms Foo has a deep knowledge in agriculture and has been in the organic food industry for the past 30 years.

Understanding the processes of giving quality organic food is important to her, even down to the fine details of knowing the type of soil and the harvesting method. She told me that one has to do his/her homework if you want to be recognized for what you do and be respected for your knowledge.

Last but not least, have faith in yourself. As mentioned earlier, the entrepreneurship path is not easy. Being confident is extremely important, but it does not mean that you get headstrong and are plain stubborn with your thoughts. Keep an open eye and open mind. Be prepared for a lot of discouragement, negative feedbacks, and people questioning and doubting you, even from those closest to you.

Follow some motivational Instagram accounts to encourage yourself daily (consider following Obstinacy Power on Instagram) because it is important to stay self-motivated.

Get my upcoming book (Obstinacy Power) if you intend to follow my proven method of achieving goals. It worked for me so many times and I am sure it will be able to help you too. I have broken down the steps to make it easy for anyone to follow. Just 6-steps!

Always remember, there is no wrong way to run a business and that you are doing it for yourself. Seek the opinion of others and talk to the right people. You only live once so live it without any regrets.

Sandra Yeow

About The Author

Sandra Yeow is a serial entrepreneur with a particular focus on the IT / Tech industry. Charismatic, passionate and motivated, Sandra overcame a difficult family background and precarious economic conditions by empowering herself through education.

Boasting a diploma in Mechatronics Engineering (2002) and a bachelor of commerce (Curtin University of Technology, 2006), Sandra ventured in the world of tech startups with a lot of energy and with an open mind. She is also a qualified Pilates instructor with Polestar Federation, as well as an author with a passion to help others achieve the full potential of their lives and careers.

Sandra is also known to be the first and only female champion for an endurance challenge in Asia –
https://en.wikipedia.org/wiki/MediaCorp_Subaru_Impreza_WRX_Challenge.

Her determination is well known to all. She believes that determination can solve every problem and situation in all aspects of life and she is sharing her strategy with everyone in her upcoming book – "Obstinacy Power - How I

Won A Car With The Power Of Determination And How You Can Win In Life & Work". For more info on her book, visit www.obstinacypower.com

Sandra is also currently building a portal to help those who want to start their own business and she hope to give some shortcuts to those who are inspired to start their own business. Visit www.sandrayeow.com to sign up for updates and keep in touch with her.

Hard Times, Creative Thinking

I started working for my father in June 2001 part-time while I was still in college. He started his custom cabinet business in 1972 with my grandfather. I was a dreamer as a kid, growing up singing in church and the school choir and starting college as a voice major. Once I realized in the middle of college that I didn't want to be an opera singer I changed my major to become an elementary school teacher. I graduated in 2002 and started the credential program and my dad asked me to stay and work for him full-time. I loved working with my dad and ultimately I decided to stay and work for him.

My job was to do the bookkeeping for the shop but I had no clue about what to do. Thankfully I had and still have a great mentor "bookkeeper" who taught me how to use Quickbooks. She also checks and fixes all my mistakes even now. From 2001 until 2006 we had some really successful years of business. It was not hard to get a job and there was plenty of work for everyone. We could pick our jobs and were always busy. My dad supervised a crew of 20 plus employees and I had plenty of work to do in the office.

Construction was hit first in the great recession and, because that affected our trade in custom wood products, we could see it turned into less sales in 2006. By 2008 when Wall Street crashed the sales were even more devastated and continued to drop. By the time people started losing their homes all around us they were not spending money on fixing their homes, they were just hoping to keep their homes.

This is when we decided to start selling cutting boards as a new source of income for the business. My dad, Mark, really pushed this idea in 2007 but I put it off for a couple of years because, after doing research on other companies' lines of cutting boards, I realised we had to make ours completely different and stand out. One day in late 2009 my dad had asked me again to try to sell cutting boards and on a whim I thought, what if we could make a cutting board in the shape of a wine bottle? And that was the beginning of an exciting adventure.

After I asked my Uncle Barry (who was working for us at the time), if he could make a cutting board in the shape of a wine bottle he said, "Sure, I'll try." And when he came into the office with this masterpiece I thought, it was pretty cool and I set it on the office counter. I didn't really know what to do after that and then I started getting comments about it from various customers and salespeople that would walk in.

One of my sales reps, Steve suggested I sell it to Williams-Sonoma. I immediately told him Williams-Sonoma owns Pottery Barn and they are way out of my league! Steve said, "No they're not, just try." I thought about it for a minute and then I got onto the internet and looked up Williams-Sonoma. I went on their website and clicked around till I found the phone number to call Mr. Williams-Sonoma.

When a "live" person answered I asked how I could submit a product for consideration in their store and she immediately connected me to a recording. The recording told me specifically to type up a one page form with the photo of my product, description, pricing, and contact info. I was happy to oblige and sent it away in the snail mail to San Francisco. I waited one week and followed up with a phone call. The girl on the other side of the phone was a little irritated with me and asked, "When did you send this submission in?" I said, "A week ago, I replied, I just wanted to follow up and see if you received it." I happily look back at how gullible I was, not knowing how all this submission stuff works. She asked me if I had listened to the entire recording, in which I replied yes and then she said, well didn't you hear it say that submissions are not responded to until 90 days later. I said, "Well, I just wanted to follow up." And she said, "Call back in 90 days." I was kind of hurt but mostly thought it was a slightly funny story so I decided to blog about it. I had only started my blog two or three months before this and I had about 7 followers.

I had no idea the phone call I would be receiving the following morning. My dad and I were talking in the office about the day's events and the phone rang…..caller I.D. said "Williams-Sonoma". I said, "Dad they must have got my submission and they're calling me!" He says, "well pick up the phone April." So I answer and the guy on the line says, "Can I please speak to April." I said, "That's me." He says, my name is Carmine, and I am a buyer for Williams-Sonoma. You are a hard person to contact April, I finally found your phone number at 10 pm last night and that was too late to call, so I'm calling you today." I said, "Well you must be calling about the submission I sent in." Carmine says, "No, I'm calling about the blog post you wrote. The president of Williams-Sonoma saw your blog post yesterday and told me to find out who you were and contact you immediately."

My heart dropped and I started to get panicky, I was back in grade school and thought I was in big trouble. Carmine continued, "I am contacting you because we think your wine bottle cutting board is excellent and we want to collaborate with you and see what you can do." I was so ecstatic, but I pretended to be cool on the phone saying, "yes"….and "ok"……and "what is your number?" Carmine said, "You're not going to put my phone number on your blog are you?" And I said, "oh no." But he had no idea I had more to blog about now!

I could not believe my blessing, this was just a small miracle of a boost in my efforts to try and get our product out in various stores.

In the following months I had planned to go to a business conference in Dallas Texas, for women. This was through E-Women Network. They had various break-out sessions and one in particular was eventful. I listened to a journalist called Lisa Johnson Mandell talk about how to get your product or idea noticed with the press, and what to expect when the press asked for more information etc. She had a lot of great insights and ideas. When the session was over I kept thinking, I need to tell her my story about Williams-Sonoma.

After the session the line was incredibly long and I waited about 20 minutes then I left the line. I went out of the room only to make myself come back and find that they were starting a new session, Lisa was leaving. I high tailed it out to the front and met Lisa there and just started talking to her. I just spat out my whole story and she said it sounded like something she would want to write about and that I should contact her after the conference. I was so grateful, I went and sat down on a comfortable seat and literally cried for the blessing of being able to tell her my story and that she would write about it.

You know what? Lisa did write about my story and it was in the AOL Jobs section on a Wednesday. By Friday Lisa had called me to tell me her boss liked the response the article got and that they wanted to put in on the front page of AOL that Saturday morning. I could not believe what I was hearing, or what was about to unfold.

This was exciting but a little nerve-wracking. While the article was on the front page my website blew up with orders for my wine bottle cutting boards, people randomly emailed me with their stories or ideas on what they wanted, and the comments section. Oh wow, that was the most interesting because I am reading all the comments of these people either congratulating me for getting my product in a retail store, or putting me down for becoming a sell-out. So many opinions, that I wanted to interject my own, but I just stayed silent. I blogged about the whole experience and it was really amazing.

A few days later I got a call at the shop from a producer at The Nate Berkus Show. She was interested in my story and wondered if I would be on the show. Of course I started crying again and then I called her. She asked me about my story and then she had to convince the other producers on the show that I should be on. It took about 3 weeks and I was literally on an airplane with my dad going to New York to be on The Nate Berkus Show. We left for New York on a Thursday and were there for only 24 hours and back home in Lodi California by Friday night. One of the most exciting opportunities was to be on that show and talk about how proud I was of my dad and his profession as a woodworker. I will never forget it.

Since the show we have had various ups and downs due to the economy we have been living in since 2008.

We built and shipped 2000 end grain wine bottle cutting boards in two months for Williams-Sonoma after the Nate Berkus Show segment aired. We shipped out many more wine bottle boards for them within the next few years. By 2011, we had created a new board, called the chef board that was put in all the top stores of Williams-Sonoma around the country. This board and the wine bottle board were discontinued after 2014 for various reasons, including a change in direction and customer demand.

I have since become a vendor with Home Goods, TJ Maxx, One Kings Lane, West Elm and others. I have a list on my cork board that shows the companies I want to do business with next to keep me motivated. I have learned from my father a lot about business but the most important one is to never give up.

Since going through the downturn in the economy I turned to my faith in Jesus to help me get through. It still gets me though that when things are going well, I should have been turning to Jesus just as often as I do in hard times. Now, every morning my dad and I pray together for the day and for God's will on our lives, and for his will on our business.

When we had to lay off all the workers we had in 2009 and it was just me and my dad. That can make you really think about the reality of the situation. But my dad's reality and mine was to never give up. God gave us just enough work to keep going, so we kept going. He gave us enough grace to get through each day and enough courage to see it through.

I will always be looking for the opportunity in the talents God has given me to keep our shop going, and to be a light in the darkness, to show others that Jesus is the Light of the World.

April Morse

About The Author

Formally known as Weber's Cabinets, now Weber Company is a small cabinet shop located in Lodi, California. We have been in business since 1972 and take pride in building a quality cabinet that can last a generation. We specialize in custom cabinetry like entertainment centers, kitchens, bathroom vanities, home offices, and much more.

We also build decorative chopping blocks, and butcher blocks currently for sale on our website and at Williams-Sonoma stores throughout the country.

We are truly a custom cabinet maker because we produce all of our cabinets and custom cutting board's right here in our Lodi shop. We also have an adjoining building which is where we finish all of our own cabinetry before it is installed.

Mark Weber started the business in 1972 with a small shop on Cherokee Lane and since has remained on Houston Lane for over 40 years. In 1998 we added on a finish shop to the right side of the shop. That gives us the ability to finish all of our work on site, which is a great asset to the company.

Mark is the brains behind the building of all our cabinetry. Mark is very talented and skilled in the area of working with wood. He won the industrial arts award upon graduation of high school and is the best in his craft. You can catch him telling his fellow employees to, "build the cabinet like it's going to go into your home. Quality and craftsmanship are always a high priority."

Mark would love for you to visit him on his blog and ask questions! Go to: www.askthecabinetmaker.com and check it out.

April Morse started working at Weber's in 2001. She is one of the Mark Weber's daughters and recently bought into the company. April wants to help in every aspect of the company including working in the shop.

She prides herself on obtaining knowledge about how the cabinets are built and what it entails. She is also learning to measure and quote jobs, and loves sales of custom products Weber's Cabinets makes. April loves working with her dad, Mark and plans on being around for a long time. April would love you to visit her on her blog at www.customcabinetgirl.com

When the economy took a turn for the worse it hit Lodi, CA very hard, particularly the construction market. Weber's Cabinets struggled. At our high point we had 25 employees. We have had multiple layoffs. As a result we decided to come up with a new product and so we started making wine-bottle shaped chopping blocks. In the beginning we sold them out of our office. Then we submitted the product to Williams-Sonoma. And we waited. April blogged about it. And then we received the call that changed the future of our company - the president of Williams-Sonoma called from Australia and said he loved our product! And now our chopping block is sold in Williams-Sonoma stores around the country.

Since then, we decided to change our company name to Weber Company because we not only produce beautiful custom cabinetry but custom cutting boards as well.

You can read about our story on AOL or see us on The Nate Berkus Show.

Thank you for your time and checking out our beautiful products!

My website; www.weber-co.com
My Blog: www.customcabinetgirl.com
Facebook: Weber Company   https://m.facebook.com/WeberCompany/
Twitter: Follow me @aprilmorse
Instagram: aprilmorse

Failing Your Way To Success

Edison once said, "I have not failed. I've just found 10,000 ways that won't work." His optimism that failure is just a step to ultimate success allowed him to keep searching for the correct materials to create an alternative to gaslight...the light bulb. No one remembers his thousands of failed attempts; they remember his success and final accomplishment which led to the invention of the light bulb.

Just as Edison failed over 9,000 times at finding the right materials for his light bulbs, I too have failed at many of the things I attempted. Just as Edison took his failures as something of pride, I use each failure as a stepping block and a learning lesson to my next attempt at something great. Failure is not something to be ashamed or afraid of, it happens to everyone, even one of the greatest inventors of all time.

Today's society puts such a negative connotation on the term "failure", as if speaking the word deserves your mouth to be washed out with soap. So many people are raised to think that failure is something to be avoided and ashamed of, not something to flaunt or embrace. The truth is that I, like many others, would not be a success and the person I am today without my failures. This is true with many of today's most successful people.

- Bill Gates failed at his first business, Traf-O-Data, and he dropped out of Harvard. He did however take his passion for computers and turned it into a career by starting Microsoft. Bill Gates is a success and no one remembers his failures.
- Vera Wang was not always a famous wedding dress designer, in fact Wang was a figure skater. When she was turned down for the US Olympic figure skating team she left and went to Vogue, then when she was turned down for the editor-in-chief position she left and became a designer. Women would never be walking down the aisle in a Vera Wang wedding gown had she made the Olympic team and competed. Her failure led to her success and some very beautiful wedding gowns.

- Colonel Saunders's secret recipe was rejected 1,000 times before anyone accepted it. He was 65 when KFC was founded. Colonel Saunders may have bloomed late in life with this success, but he was a success and he never gave up.
- Thirty-six publishers rejected Arianna Huffington's second book before she got finally got it published. She eventually went and launched The Huffington Post, and we all know how well she is doing today. If she didn't let 36 publishers shut her down, then you shouldn't let one rejection get in your way.
- Mark Cuban failed as a carpenter, cook and even a waiter. He says of his failures, "I've learned that it doesn't matter how many times you failed. You only have to be right once. I tried to sell powdered milk. I was an idiot lots of times, and I learned from them all." Today Mark Cuban is one of the most successful businessmen in America and he too credits his success to his failures.

As a student in school I had a hard time with achieving good grades, my failures (literally) prevented me from driving until I was 18 years old. My parents had a strict policy that driving is a privilege, not a right, and my grades had to be high enough to receive a privilege such as driving. I was 18 years old and my 16-year-old sister drove me around. Talk about embarrassing! My failure to get to drive in high school forced me to learn new study techniques and test taking methods, these new skills would help me achieve better grades in college. Remember, in college, you don't lose the privilege to drive when you fail, you lose the privilege to take classes. I eventually became so skilled at studying and taking tests that the university I attended hired me to tutor other students in specific subjects and show them how to take notes and take tests effectively. My experience of failing classes in high school led me to work harder in school and eventually led to me getting paid to teach others my methods. If I hadn't failed so early on, the opportunity to teach and tutor may have never been and option.

Once I graduated from college the failures really started to stack up. I couldn't find a job for the first 6 months I was out of school. Even with a college degree and having worked 5 jobs while in college, no one wanted to hire a recent college graduate. Failing to be hired for all the jobs I applied for, I went into retail and started selling purses at the local mall for a high-end purse line. I kept applying for jobs even while in retail and continued to get rejected but the experiences I learned in retail have benefitted me greatly. I learned how to work with a team of girls (not easy at times), I increased my sales abilities and I learned better customer service. The skills I learned working retail have proven to be more valuable than I could have ever imagined when I first started at a $9/hour job.

After two years of applying and working in bars, restaurants and retail I was finally given the opportunity to do something I was good at; marketing. An international manufacturer offered me the marketing director position, the job of a lifetime. Prior to accepting the position I asked them why they were hiring me (which in hindsight was a stupid thing to do). I told them I had no marketing experience, I had less than a year of management experience, I had never had a corporate job and I knew nothing about their products. So why were they hiring me? The response by the president has been embedded in my mind since that day in September 2012. She said, "Samantha, you fail at so many things that you attempt and try. You fail a lot...but you get back up every time and that is why we need you at our company. We need someone who is resilient". Resilient. I had never heard myself described that way but she was right. I did attempt many new projects, jobs and adventures only to have things fall through, not happen or not work out. I wasn't a failure at life; I was resilient.

Failure is defined in Merriam-Webster's dictionary as "lack of success", but I don't see it that way. Failure is not a lack of success; failure is success at discovering something that didn't work. If you look at failure as something that happens to everyone, something that is inevitable in life and something that you can learn from, then failure is nothing to be afraid of or avoid.

When you fail at something use it as a learning experience, observe your mistakes, analyse what went wrong and determine what you will do differently next time. As long as you don't make the same mistake again, your errors and failures are nothing more than just a learning opportunity. You can never learn what is right if you don't know what is wrong and you can't learn what is wrong without making mistakes.

Failing is a good thing. Yes, a good thing and nothing to be afraid of. One of the most over looked reasons why we must embrace failure is that it prevents arrogance and a pompous attitude that often comes over those who have consistent and constant success. When you mess up and have to try again you are more proud of the final outcome and your success. In short, failing makes you less egotistical. Failure makes people humble.

I remember many times, while I was managing the marketing department at the international manufacturer, when I proposed a new marketing strategy or campaign and it was shut down. Quite often they didn't even read the entire report just said "no" instantly. Rather than going back to my cubical and crying or getting upset, I got creative. I found new ways to show the rest of the board just why my idea and plan was good, effective and the right decision. Oftentimes it was the proposals that I initially had shut down and had to get creative on that did the best. Failure encourages you to think creatively and come up with new alternatives.

When you experience a failure it's simply an indication that there is something else out there that will work better and bring higher success. Failure brings new opportunities that you may have never thought of. If I had been hired right out of college into my dream job then I may have never gone into retail and bartending, thus I would have never had the opportunity to learn better sales and customer service skills. As cliché as it sounds, everything happens for a reason and failure isn't the end of the road, it's the reason to keep pushing forward.

I was fired within my 90 days from what I thought was going to be my career for decades. I was never told why I was fired but remembering the wise words of the manufacturing firm's president "you're resilient", I wasted no time moping and feeling sorry for myself. Rather, I made a phone call and had a new job in less than 30 minutes. I don't like to promote the fact that I was fired at the age of 27, but I was and I don't let it get me down. Losing the job I thought was perfect for me opened more doors than I could have ever fathomed. I learned from that termination that I am a leader and that my ability to take initiative and be a go-getter was something to be proud of, not suppressed. A few short months after being fired I left the corporate world to pursue my company full time and have never looked back. The ultimate failure, job termination, was in fact a blessing and I wish I could thank that manager for letting me go from the company, they did me a huge favor.

Every time I failed at something I learned something new about myself. Failing allows you to discover the real you. Sometimes we get complacent in our jobs, careers and places in life and just accept things as they are. If we hit a bump in the road such as a termination or other negative aspect of life, we are jostled and brought back to the real world. This is a good thing and often necessary throughout life. Failing reminds you to stay on your toes, not to slack and it allows your true colors to come out. Only in the darkest of times will the true you really come to fruition. How would you handle a failure, termination or other roadblock at this point in your life?

Finally, going back to Edison's wise words he once said, "Many of life's failures are people who did not realize how close they were to success when they gave up". Don't give up just because you failed, use that failure as momentum to learn and keep pushing forward.

Samantha R. Strazanac

About The Author

Samantha R. Strazanac resides in Raleigh, North Carolina where she runs her marketing consulting firm, Strazanac Solutions with her Chihuahua, Caly, by her side. Samantha has a degree in Psychology and Leadership from Western Carolina University in Cullowhee, NC and graduated in 2010.

She enjoys ballroom dancing, cooking and spending time with her family, friends and dog. Samantha has worked in retail, veterinary medicine, dance, as a tutor, a wedding planner, in medical sales, media sales, kitchen good sales and even trade show planning but none of those jobs were right for her.

Throughout her life Samantha had aspirations to be a veterinarian, pharmaceutical representative, marketing executive, media sales executive and events professional, but life threw other things her way and through all her failure attempts at those careers she is now happier than ever. She credits her success to her multiple attempts at looking for the right fit when all she needed to do was wait for the right fit to develop on its own.

Website: www.strazanacsolutions.com

Twitter: @StrazSolutions

Facebook: https://www.facebook.com/strazanacsolutions/

Email: samantha@strazanacsolutions.com

18539620R00135

Printed in Great Britain
by Amazon